REAL
WORLD
FAITH

WALTER BRUEGGEMANN

REAL WORLD FAITH

Foreword
Erskine Clarke

Fortress Press
Minneapolis

REAL WORLD FAITH

Library of Congress Control Number: 2023932816 (print)

Cover design: John Lucas
Cover image: Bokeh photography of city lights during night time, Photo by
ibuki Tsubo on Unsplash

Print ISBN: 978-1-5064-9267-4
eBook ISBN: 978-1-5064-9268-1

CONTENTS

Part IV
War and Peace

Part V
Reflections More Personal

FOREWORD

It is often said that Walter Brueggemann is the nation's most influential biblical scholar. This perception reflects the respect—indeed the awe—of other scholars who gladly claim him as a colleague. But his influence, of course, goes far beyond the academy and its important concerns. Where his influence has been most deeply felt is among the theologians of the church, the faithful pastors who week by week interpret for congregations the Word of God as it confronts our "Real World," and among the congregations who hear him quoted directly or hear his interpretive insights embedded in sermons, in church classes, in pastoral care, and in the church's ministry to a hurting world. The church is Brueggemann's "natural habitat," and in his Introduction to this present volume he says that his recurring effort "is to try to open the biblical text through exposition that may serve in critical ways to empower the church in its life and mission."

Any reader of Brueggemann knows his astonishing knowledge of biblical texts, how he moves with ease and stunning insights among familiar and often obscure—to the rest of us—texts to focus on a particular concern or theme. The biblical texts all seem to be his old friends among whom he has spent a lifetime asking questions of them and being questioned by them. And he asks these old friends questions that few of us would ever think of asking and he hears questions from them that most of us are too deaf or preoccupied to hear. It is this asking and hearing conversation that he has shared with us over many years and that has been such a gift to the life of the church.

Brueggemann, however, has invited others into the conversation; indeed, the biblical texts themselves have insisted that he invite others into the conversation as the texts confront our "Real World." Again, any reader of Brueggemann will know the astonishing breadth of his reading, not only biblical studies but also novels, history, sociology, cultural studies, psychology and philosophy, political commentaries, and on and on. All of these are brought into his conversation with biblical texts and with the Holy One encountered in the texts.

But Brueggemann also invites us into this conversation. He invites us to question and be questioned by the biblical texts and by those studies of our "Real World." His invitation is for the sake of the church's life and mission and to a glad and faithful obedience to the One who is Lord of the church. The conversation, he says, which is at the "interface of faith and life," is not one that ends at the conclusion of a church service or study group but is "open-ended and never finished" because the "Spirit is always unsettling our best conclusion."

So this volume is a gracious invitation into this larger conversation. As a collection of discrete yet related essays, each of modest length, it can be especially helpful to faithful preachers busy with many aspects of the church's common life and to others eager to think about how faith relates to pressing issues of contemporary life. And not incidentally, it provides splendid examples of Brueggemann's own ongoing conversation that has been such a gift to the church. Chapter titles provide hints of particular subjects addressed in that conversation: "There Are Conspiracies and Then There Are Conspiracies," "Habeas Corpus," "Speak Truth; Do Justice," "The Strangeness of the Stranger," and on and on, thirty-one essays altogether plus an introduction and conclusion. *Real World Faith* is consequently another gift Walter Brueggemann offers to the church, a gift forged in his own faithful attention to his calling, and a gift we eagerly unwrap in anticipation of being surprised and encouraged by Good News.

Erskine Clarke

INTRODUCTION

It turns out that blogs are just the right genre for an old man who still has a lively critical thought, but lacks the energy for extended exposition. For that reason I am glad to have been able to write these several pieces originally published in 2021 and 2022, and glad that I may share them more broadly in this collection. My grounding, as always, is in the exposition of the biblical text. And the natural habitat for my work is the church in which I am a critical insider. Thus my effort, recurringly, is to try to open the biblical text through exposition that may serve in critical ways to empower the church in its life and mission. My assumption is that most readers of my blogs at Church Anew (https://churchanew.org) are engaged church members, many of whom are pastors. I take that company as my natural readership, and so my writing is an effort at collegiality with those who care about gospel faith and who seek to live it out in ways that make a difference. I belong—not surprisingly—to a theological tradition rooted in Calvin, shaped by German pietism, and mediated through Reinhold Niebuhr among others, that believes that the claims of *gospel faith* voiced in the Bible concern our *common life* and the practice of *civic responsibility*. Thus my intent here is to support the rich and varied ways in which our faith impinges on our common public life.

The organization of these materials here is more than a bit arbitrary, but hopefully the five parts into which the book is divided will aid the reader in following my general line of thinking. I have placed several pieces concerning the church in part I, both because of my readership and because of my own glad habitat in the church. I have considered several aspects of church life and practice, always with an eye on the ways in which the fresh challenges we face summon us in ways that never come without some risk.

The preoccupation of the church with the reality of suffering and pain in the world has led me in part II to consider some instances of social pain among us. Our current season of fear and anxiety (that tilts us toward exclusivism for our own kind) compels us to think of and notice especially the "stranger" who is welcomed in the gospel. Of course this welcome pertains particularly toward the "stranger" of another "race." And this as our society now is much bent toward racism and white supremacy.

This accent on social pain, and the chance to redeem that pain, has pressed upon me a number of civic issues in part III. These issues concern the role and size of government, the glue of friendship that makes democracy work, and our current exclusionary practices that want to deny membership to some who feel like a threat to our preferred social arrangements.

Part IV singles out, from more general civic concerns, the crisis of war and peace in which we are now embroiled, and in which we are endlessly entangled in our national posturing, along with our imagined exceptionalism. That national preoccupation permits us to further imagine that the Holy One is on our side, while at the same time wanting to disregard the restraints that the Holy One imposes everywhere in creation.

Part V is more or less random, in which I have included some commentary of a more personal kind, most especially concerning our beloved cat, Sammy. It turns out (see chapter 30: Reprise for Sammy) that our beloved cat has embodied and continues to represent the truth of our dialogic existence. I have included here as well a critical tribute to Norman Gottwald from whom I have learned "most and best."

I have settled on the title for this collection, *Real World Faith*. That is, this collection is among our main attempts to articulate faith that is effectively linked to our real world, the world of our bodies and the body politic. (On this accent, see my book, *Materiality as Resistance: Five Elements for Moral Action in the Real World* [2020].) The real world of our bodies causes us to be largely preoccupied with our health, security, dignity, and sexuality, and causes us concern for food and shelter, for us and for our neighbors. The real world of the body politic puts us in inescapable touch with issues of money, power, weapons, policies, treaties, taxes, and trade agreements. These are the matters that occupy us most of the time on most of our days. They are the proper agenda of our faith because our faith consists in trust in the One who governs our bodily life in the world. Our interpretive work is to try to articulate the ways—albeit hidden ways—in which the agency and character of God makes effective contact with our world. This is "real-life faith."

In all of these reflective pieces I bear witness in two ways. First, they all attest to the rich and compelling ways in which our *faith matters* to the practice of our common life. But second, they attest that the work is *open-ended and never finished*. Thus the ongoing project of interpretation that lives at the interface of faith and life continues to press upon us. It is work that on the one hand refuses to settle for any "final solution" of interpretation that we especially treasure because the Spirit is always unsettling our best conclusion. On the other hand, our ongoing interpretive work, when we have courage and wisdom, may always impinge upon our common life in significant ways that continue to empower and perplex us.

I am especially glad to thank Mary Brown, who has invited me to her blog platform, Church Anew, where I have been able to continue my work. Mary is endlessly attentive and generous. And I am grateful to Carey Newman at Fortress Press who has agreed to edit and publish this collection, a happy affirmation for me since my connection with Fortress Press goes back to ancient days, all of which are filled with gratitude for the long succession of editors at the press. In the same way, my links to Carey are long-running, so I am grateful to him. Most especially I am grateful to Tia Brueggemann who has proofed and edited every syllable of this manuscript. Without her attentiveness I would not have gotten this into print. It is my hope that this collection will serve as a support and resources for many colleagues who take their faith with straight-up seriousness. These friends and colleagues matter a great deal, and I am glad to be in solidarity with them.

PRAYER
Life Outside Our Homemade Cages

(On reading John 9)

We live conveniently in our homemade cages of explanation.
We live comfortably in our cages of cause and effect.
> *We liberals live in our cages of being smarter and more*
> > *woke;*
> *We conservatives live in our cages of being better grounded*
> *and more reliable.*
In our cages of ideology, we sense our control,
> *our ability to explain,*
> *our capacity to link cause to effect,*
> > *to connect deed to consequence.*

Our cages are self-justifying; we never question them, and the
> *world is made morally sensible.*
We win the blame game every time!
> *We reason backward from consequence to deed*
> > *from effect to cause;*
> > *our arithmetic never fails us.*

But then sometimes—not often—but often enough
> *Your wonders elude our explanations;*
> *Your miracles violate our confident calculations.*
> *Once in a while . . .*
> > *healing breaks through,*
> > *generosity overwhelms our arithmetic,*
> > *forgiveness moves beyond our reasoning,*
> > *hospitality exposes our careful management.*

Beyond our expectation
  comes your freighted holiness:
    new sight for the blind,
    new walking for the lame,
    new hearing for the deaf,
    new possibility for the poor,
      new freedom, new wellbeing, new joy,
  all beyond our caged explanations.

Your holiness breaks our numbness;
Your holiness mocks our moral control;
Your holiness opens life beyond our blame games.
We pause in awe before your transformative power.
  We move beyond our management;
    we mount up with wings like eagles,
      we run in eagerness and are not tired;
        we walk in wellbeing and do not grow faint.

We are made new well beyond our best selves.
It is no surprise that we break out in loud praise,
  lost in wonder at your goodness,
  lost in love for the new world you give,
  Lost in praise for you . . . you . . . you alone! Amen.

Part I

THE CHURCH IN ITS LIFE AND MISSION

BARMEN AGAIN?

THE DRAFT COURT opinion written by Justice Alito concerning *Roe v. Wade* is no doubt an important step in our society toward fascism—or some other less-named form of authoritarianism. Whereas the historical function of the Supreme Court has been to protect individual liberty from the incursion of the states, the Alito opinion does just the opposite; it invites the ruthless incursion of the state into individual lives and personal matters. It does so, moreover, at the behest of a small minority against the better judgment of the great majority of our citizens. It is the imprint of state control on the most intimate personal dimensions of our human life.

The forthcoming court ruling may be an important wake-up call to the church and its pastors. While there are and will be disagreements concerning "pro-life" and "pro-choice" positions, there can hardly be disagreement about the incursion of the state into a zone of human freedom and responsibility. We may pause over the question and answer of the *Heidelberg Catechism*:

> *What is your only comfort, in life and in death?*
> *That I belong—body and soul, in life and in death—*
> *not to myself but to my faithful Savior, Jesus Christ . . .*

The full answer in the catechism is more extended, but the key phrase is, "I belong not to myself but to Jesus Christ." In our present context, the answer might also have said, "I belong not to the state, but to Jesus Christ." That affirmation of course is a Christian confession that many others may not make. It is, nonetheless, the claim of our faith that whether we confess Christ or not, we are—all of us!—creatures who receive life from the creator, live our lives back to the creator, and belong to our creator. It is the claim of our faith that we are creatures well beloved by the creator, created by God *ex nihilo*, or as Norman Wirzba has said so well, *creatio ex amore*, out of nothing . . . out of love. Such beloved creatures do not and cannot belong to the state, and cannot have the state making claims on our bodies that are gifts from God. Thus it is striking that the catechism affirms that we belong to God, "body and soul." It is a stunning act of hubris for the state to imagine that it can properly control our bodies and mandate their performance.

This crisis moment in the long history of court rulings, a moment in which the court proposes to take away from us an elemental right, may be an alert to the church that we may be ready to teach and preach the most elemental claims of our faith in a way that clarifies the deep either/or of faith: Either we belong to our creator God, or we belong to the state that can accordingly command our lives and our bodies. We may not render to Caesar what we properly render to God.

It is my thought that this will be a very good and important time for pastors and teachers in the church to reintroduce the church to the *Barmen Declaration* that has been largely forgotten among us. The reason for this thinking is that the Barmen Declaration is the most important act in the church in recent time that staked out the elemental claims for the gospel in opposition to disastrous idolatrous distraction, an act that has been boldly reiterated in the *Kairos Document* and in the *Belhar Confession* in South Africa. The Barmen Declaration, written in 1934, largely by Karl Barth, was a confessional, confessing act whereby the church in Germany sought to assert its gospel truth in opposition to the false claims of National Socialism. The declaration contains six paragraphs, each of which is introduced by a *scriptural citation*, and each of which makes a *frontal affirmation* with a concluding *sharp rejection* linked to the affirmation. The declaration is easily and readily critiqued because it reflects a certain mode of German theology geared to a particular historical crisis and, most notably, it is silent concerning the fate of Jews in Germany. Given those problems with the declaration, it is nonetheless a bold act of faith that joins issue with the false claims of the state in Germany. It is to be noted that the Kairos Document in South Africa in like manner includes a sharp critique of "state theology."

Given the strength and energy of "state theology" in the United States now, reflected in Alito's opinion, it is important for church members in the United States to be educated about Barmen, Behlar, and the Kairos Document, to be made aware of the way in which Christians elsewhere in our lifetime have faced idolatrous regimes in their particular contexts. My sense is that most church members in the United States little suspect this sharp edge to the life and faith of the church, and little understand the risks that our contemporaries have run for the truth of the gospel. For the most part, church theology in the United States is accommodationist, and church practice is keenly domesticated to fit in easily with state theology. And now the draft court ruling is an indication of the ways in which state theology has grown in energy and boldness, sadly and pathetically supported in uncritical ways by many who claim to speak for the church.

This moment of crisis requires determined political action. But it also requires that the church do critical thinking about our faith after the US church has been easily domesticated for a long time. While the actions to be undertaken among us are not very clear at the moment— at least to me—it is certainly a teaching moment. Thus it is my modest proposal that the church should again be introduced to confessional language and confessional thinking so that the church members can be alerted to the crisis of faith into which we are placed when the state claims for itself regulation of our lives that belong to our creator God. This would of course be a disruptive wake-up call for many in the church who regard the church as a benign adjunct to an otherwise friendly, conformist life.

Such teaching after Barmen would consider the dangerous context of the church in Germany already in 1934, long before we in the United States had even noticed the rise of National Socialism. But it would also offer instruction,

- in the *bold appeal to Scripture* as is done in the declaration, Scripture that makes deep, nonnegotiable claims on our lives;
- in the *theological articulation of freedom and responsibility* in the gospel that pertain to our moment of faith, freedom, and responsibility that belongs to the oldest paradigm of *Exodus* (a refusal of the state authority of Pharaoh) and *Sinai* (glad obedience to the God of emancipation), but also to Jesus's call to *discipleship*;
- in the *rejection of idolatry* that concludes each part of the declaration, idolatry that claims an ultimacy for itself that can only belong to God.

Such pastoral education would invite contemporary church members—especially young people—into the recent history of the church and into the ways in which the church thinks gladly, boldly, and faithfully in its political context.

I have said nothing here about abortion or "pro choice," or any of the specifics that are addressed in the Alito opinion. Surely it is beyond debate that such matters of reproduction belong properly to the most intimate conversation between a mother and her doctor, and at best the father. Urgent political action is required among us.

But the larger stake that must concern us in the church at the same time is nothing less than the Lordship of Christ, the Lord of freedom and responsibility. The rule of the God of the gospel has always been in vigorous contestation with would-be alternatives. We know this in our own time with the rise of lethal authoritarian regimes. We also know this in Scripture with the familiar procession of Pharaoh, Sennacherib, Nebuchadnezzar, even Cyrus and, eventually, Caesar. The nexus point of Good Friday pitted the rule of God over against the rule of Caesar. For an instant late on Friday, the mighty force of Caesar prevailed, but then, amid that seeming victory for the empire, came the inexplicable, nonnegotiable reality of Easter newness. It turns out then and thereafter that the governance of the world is wrested away from the rule of Caesar and belongs to the creator God who wills wellbeing for all creatures, quite apart from the coercive claim of Caesar.

So let the local congregation ponder the Lordship of Christ, not the Lordship of "this world," and not the Lordship of some remote alternative, but the Lordship of Christ that is breaking out in the "fruits of the spirit" everywhere every day. It turns out that "the Lordship of Christ" is not a sentimental mantra, but rather a serious public claim that deabsolutizes every other claim, including the one championed by Alito. The Barmen Declaration is a good place from which to think about the Lordship of Christ in terms of social specificity. Engaged in such reflective study, the church might recover for itself some of the great hymns of the church that bespeak the rule of God that have been shelved in the interest of privatized sentimentality. As the gospel writers came to see, confrontation with the coercive power of the state is no dress rehearsal or practice session. It is the real thing. It is the real thing to be able to say that our "only comfort" is that we belong "body and soul" to our faithful savior.

I do not imagine that pastors or congregations are prepared for heroic action. This, I judge, is not a time for heroic action. Rather, it is a time for reflection, with sober honest discipline, on the claims of our faith that places us (as it always does) in crisis and invites us to a fresh sense of wellbeing as we claim "our only comfort in life and in death."

The Heidelberg Catechism finishes with instruction concerning the Lord's Prayer. It ends with the "Amen" of the prayer:

Amen means: this shall truly and certainly be. For my prayer is much more certainly heard by God than I am persuaded in my heart that I desire such things from him.

In support of this wondrous statement the catechism quotes II Corinthians 1:20:

> *All the promises of God find their Yes in him. That is why we*
> *utter Amen through him, to the glory of God.*

The divine utterance of such a "yes" is emancipatory in our present circumstance, giving us freedom for boldness in the face of coercive idolatry.

2

ON SACRAMENTAL PRONOUNS

AS A REGULAR churchgoer, I love to fall back into the familiar phrase and cadences of the liturgy. While I am a low church Protestant, I have great appreciation for the recital of the classical liturgy. I take its familiar words as expansive poetic articulation of the mystery of faith, and so do not worry very much about the specificities. I take the sum of the liturgical cadences to be much more than the sum of its parts that I do not stop to parse.

My long practice of liturgy with access to a variety of ecclesial articulations, however, did not prepare me for the quite unexpected crisis in the liturgy reported in our local paper. On February 17, 2022, the *Record-Eagle* reported a piece from Phoenix entitled, "Baptisms by Arizona Priest Presumed Invalid Due to Error." The report concerned Father Andres Arango who served as a priest in Arizona for sixteen years. During that time he regularly baptized new believers with the formula, "We baptize you in the name of the Father, of the Son, and of the Holy Spirit." In my Free Church tradition, we might have quibbled about the use of the Trinitarian formula! But in the less humorous response of the Catholic Church, the objection ("error!") concerns the use of the plural pronoun "we" that, according to the Vatican, made all the baptisms of Father Arango invalid. The church insists on the singular pronoun, "I baptize." So now, the paper reports, there is an eager effort to identify all of those wrongly baptized who must be rebaptized.

Just five days later (February 22, 2022), the *Record-Eagle* had a second story on the case entitled, "Botched Baptisms Roiled Michigan Church?" It turns out that this same priest, Andres Arango, was previously a priest in Troy, Michigan, and regularly used the same mistaken baptismal formula with a plural pronoun. Thus in Michigan or in Arizona, the church has had to be busy rectifying the priestly "error."

I must confess I was not and am not alarmed about the plural pronoun. It seems just right to me. In the first article it is reported that the "errant priest" was using the plural pronoun to make baptism "more of a communal affair including parents, godparents and the community," with the purpose of "welcoming a new member into the church." OMG! Who would have thought baptism could be a "communal affair," and who would ever have contemplated that it was a welcome to a new member into the community of faith? I judge that only the most reactionary scholastics would be affronted by such contemplation. In the second article the explanation of the "error" is even less compelling. "It is not the 'we' of the congregation doing the baptizing, but the 'I' of Jesus Christ, acting through the priest and deacon, that makes a baptism valid." That seems to me a remarkably novel mode of reasoning. After all, Jesus never baptized anyone! If one reads about the mass baptisms by Peter in the book of Acts, moreover, I hazard that Peter had no sacramental awareness that he was acting in the role of Jesus Christ. It is not Jesus who welcomes folk into the church. It is the church that does the welcome through its ministry. The only conclusion that I could draw is that the hierarchy of the church wants to protect and underscore the singular authority of the priest who controls the sacrament. Thus the debate appears to arise from a concern to protect and maintain authority, power, privilege, and preeminence. The objection is odd since the bishops of the church have not hesitated, for a long time, to use the "royal we" in their pronouncements. And when they do, the "mystery of faith" is crowded out by the "mystery of the church."

This all strikes me as an absurd fluff about very little. It is nonetheless an opportunity to think afresh about the communal nature of the Christian congregation and of the need for a "rightly ordered" ministry. I have no doubt that a "rightly ordered" ministry is essential for the church, but as a low church pastor, I regard that as a *functional* requirement and not as an *ontological* reality. Of course, this is an old quibble in the church, and arguments are long mustered on both sides of it. It is hard for me, nonetheless, to imagine that a "mistaken" pronoun in the recital of the liturgy could lead to a frantic effort to identify its "victims" as candidates for rebaptism. After all, in cases of emergency, anyone can baptize. And every time it happens, the one who baptizes acts in and for the whole church. It is this common conviction concerning baptism that is at the root of all ecumenical possibility!

Thus we might rightly reflect, yet again, on Paul's great articulation of *the unity of the church* and the requirement of *a variety of gifts* for a well-ordered ministry within that community. Our reasoning might include three moves. First, Paul's great accent on *the unity of the Body of the church*. This imagery of the body means that every member, every element of the church, is important and has a role to play. That of course is why we sing in the church:

> We *share each other's woes, our mutual burdens bear;*
> *and often for each other flows the sympathizing tear.*
> > ("Blessed be the Tie that Binds")

We are indeed bound together and to each other in deep caring dimensions that go well beneath our reasoning. Or in a hymn we no longer sing in the church because of its martial imagery:

> We *are not divided, all one body* we,
> *one in hope and doctrine, one in charity.*
> > ("Onward Christian Soldiers")

What better than to be "one in doctrine, confessing the same narrative, one in hope" that is best expressed in lyrical imagination. And one in charity, being generously grateful together. Or together we lean on the everlasting arms that make us altogether "safe and secure." It is a fellowship!

> *What a fellowship, what a joy divine, leaning on the everlasting*
> *   arms;*
> *What a blessedness, what a peace is mine,*
> *Leaning on the everlasting arms, leaning, leaning,*
> *safe and secure from all alarms, leaning on the everlasting arms.*
>   ("Leaning on the Everlasting Arms")

We could imagine, in such a fellowship of solidarity, that we might say "we" to welcome new members!

But second, Paul is careful, in his extended articulation, to identify and take seriously very distinctive roles and functions in the church that he terms "a variety of gifts, a variety of services, and a variety of activities" (I Corinthians 12:4–5). He names some of these roles and functions; we may believe that his list is representative and not exhaustive. Thus we may imagine that over time the church might require many different roles and functions in order to perform the future of the whole body. Thus no doubt room is made for ministers who baptize, who are entrusted with that responsibility as one of a variety of gifts.

Thus Paul articulates both the claim of the whole body and the function of the parts. Paul does not and apparently does not need to sort out all of this. As a result, the two sides of Paul's argument are left as the endlessly continuing work of the church to adjudicate the claims of community and leadership. While the Reformation, at least in theory if not in practice, made great claims for the priesthood of all, the catholic (small "c") tradition makes large claims for the specificity of priestly leadership as a requirement for the "right order" of the body. No doubt the baptismal matter concerning the work of Father Arango in Arizona and Michigan reflects the ongoing adjudication of the matter. And I, as a low church Protestant, must make room for the fact that adjudication of the work of Father Arango may conclude there was an "error" that requires correction.

But what I find most important is that Paul makes a third move in his delineation of the church, a third move that does not figure in the anxious response of the church to Father Arango's well-intended priestly actions. At the end of I Corinthians 12, Paul returns to the specific roles in the church to which he has earlier alluded (27–30). But his exposition does not end there. In verse he speaks of "greater gifts" and then uses his wondrous familiar phrase, "a still more excellent way." With this breathtaking formulation, chapter 12 spills over into chapter 13. It turns out that I Corinthians 13 is not a "love chapter" designed for weddings. It is rather the completion of Paul's reasoning about the nature of the church, its unity, and its variety of gifts. I take it that Paul himself is aware that he has left unsettled the tension between *the one body* and the variety of gifts. And now, in this lyrical chapter, he shows the church how to adjudicate the quandary of one body and *the variety of gifts*. The "still more excellent way" is the way of self-giving love. My sense is that in this exuberant affirmation of the self-giving love singularly evident in Jesus, Paul regards the adjudication of one body and a variety of gifts as a moot and uninteresting question. I remember back in the early days of television on a show entitled "What's My Line?," after a back and forth of score keeping participants, the emcee would simply void the scorekeeping, and flip the chart of points to completion. So Paul simply flips the scorekeeping of the church to completion in chapter 13. What counts, in Paul's horizon, is not whether the variety of gifts is more important than the one body, or vice versa. Both fade in importance before the summons and force of *agape* that the church is to perform. In the wake of such reasoning that ends in self-giving, I conclude that the Lord of baptism will not want to quibble over pronouns. Presumably, we may take it that Father Arango acted in love toward those whom he baptized. Further, those who witnessed the baptisms could see for themselves that Father Arango acted in such love. Give or take a pronoun, that is what mattered in the baptisms and what continues to matter.

I have no particular stake in how the Catholic Church settles the question posed by Father Arango. I have no special interest in this quandary that the church has manufactured for itself. But it does interest me that in the wake of chapter 12, Paul's chapter 13 is always calling the church back to its core business, away from its particular quarrels and its tendency to forget its nature and work. The single business of the church, as in Paul, is to embrace a "still more excellent way." Or as H. Richard Niebuhr has said it, "The work of the church is to increase the love of God and of neighbor." This "still more excellent way" will guide the Methodist Church in Michigan where I am a member in its current quarrel concerning sexuality. This "still more excellent way" clearly will assist the church in its regular adjudication of budgets, buildings, and programs.

Paul goes on in chapter 14 to speak of "building up" the church (vv. 5, 12). In the end he urges that things in the church be done "decently and in order" (14:40), but not in ways that detract from the up-building to be done in *agape*. Pronouns matter; they do not matter ultimately. I can imagine that the "I" of the priest and the "we" of the community converge together for the up-building of a community of *agape*. The test of a pronoun is what "builds up." Our usual quarrels and our quibbles about pronouns do not at all build up. It remains for the community of the baptized to get on with up-building through the variety of gifts entrusted to the church. We do that when we are one in hope, one in doctrine, but above all, one in charity (*agape*).

3

SEEING MORE THAN TREES

ONE OF MY best Christmas presents is a book from my son and his wife, *The Lincoln Highway* by Amor Towles (2021). Wonderful storyteller that he is, Towles takes us on a lively meandering venture from rural Nebraska (where my roots are) to New York City (where I studied). Protagonists in the narrative are two brothers, the older Emmett, the younger Billy. Billy is a genuine, most discerning innocent. He has been smitten by a book he has read twenty-five times, namely, *Compendium of Heroes, Adventurer, and other Intrepid Followers.* The book, in short chapters, features adventurers from mythology (most especially Ulysses), plus noted inventors, people who lived life large and made a difference.

For Billy a high point of the story occurred when he, along with Woolley, Duchess, and Ulysses, went to the fifty-fifth floor of the Empire State Building and met with the noted Professor Abernathe, author of Billy's treasured book. Amid their conversation with the genial affirming author, Abernathe delivered this most compelling oration that I take to be the most interesting paragraph in the entire book. He said:

> But having confessed that I have lived my life through books,
> I can at least report that I have done so with conviction.
> Which is to say, Mr. Ulysses, that I have read a great deal. I
> have read thousands of books, many of them more than once.
> I have read histories and novels, scientific tracts and volumes
> of poetry. And from all of these pages upon pages, one thing
> I have learned is that there is just enough variety in human
> experience for every single person in a city the size of New

York to feel with assurance that their experience is unique.
And this is a wonderful thing. Because to aspire, to fall in
love, to stumble as we do and yet soldier on, at some level we
must believe that what we are going through has never been
*experienced quite as **we** have experienced it.* (560)

Because, like the professor, I have read a great deal, I have paused over this paragraph. It is for certain that reading can bring before us the rich variety and specificity of human experience. But beyond that we see, with the professor, that every human life is distinctive, and every human experience is unique. It is that distinctiveness and uniqueness that make for good storytelling, good imagining, good preaching, and good living. In Towles's narrative it is the ancient myth of Ulysses that permits Billy to assign to his contemporary large, dark friend, also named Ulysses, a dimension of hope whereby he is freshly empowered to a new life after a life of failure and defeat.

Then I began to think about every human life being different, and every human experience being unique. It is so for every parent of a first child, for every kid coming home from college after the first semester, every high school athletic champion. Never before *such a baby*, never before *such a semester*, never before *such a victory*! My attention turned to the short narrative in Mark 8:22–26 in which Jesus meets a blind beggar. Jesus administers an ancient, Elisha-like remedy of saliva to the blind man (see II Kings 4:34, 5:10). Then the blind man can discern movement and shapes. But he still could not distinguish them. They all looked alike. They all looked like maples, or oaks, or cedars: "I can see people that look like trees walking." The man is on his way to seeing. And then, "Jesus laid his hands on his eyes again." Mark narrates: "He looked intently and his sight was restored." He was looking intently like we do in a vision test to see the smallest print we can read. And then, we are told, "He saw everything clearly." Mark uses a term that is nowhere else deployed in the New Testament, "Plainly, clearly." He could see actual folks. He could identify specific persons.

His grudging blur had been overcome! All that had been required for his restoration was the ancient application of saliva and the transformative touch of Jesus!

It occurred to me that for the most part we see "people walking like trees." We see them as statistics that lack specificity, identity, or claim upon us. We readily use our social-scientific skills to economize; we group and categorize and stereotype. We do that with people whom we do not know. And we do it with people whom we fear. For a long time, of course, we whites have just in that way categorized Blacks. They all look alike, like trees! It is easier to group those whom we do not know and whom we fear and then easier to dismiss them, denying them their rights and access, or eventually denying them their humanity. We do not have then to bother with them!

That of course is why stories count for so much. Stories are particular to time, place, context, circumstance, and person. Stories cannot be summarized. The blind man first could only see trees. Only later, after *the touch*, could he identify and name individuals. John O'Banion, in *Reorienting Rhetoric* (1987), has shown how our knowledge and perception are tilted either toward "stories" that specify or toward "lists" that summarize and dismiss. We tell stories of that which we treasure; we make lists of that which is alien to us. Jesus enacted stories but refused lists. Jesus made it possible for this blind man to enter the rich inventory of stories, no longer enthralled to summarizing lists of maples, oaks, and cedars. He saw, rather, *this* tree, *this* person and, eventually, *this* neighbor!

I do not suggest that the touch of Jesus and the reading of the professor are equivalents. They are quite different in their claims. It is nonetheless the case that wide, deep, careful reading does indeed help us to see the multivariants of creaturely life in all its richness. When we are not reading regularly outside our comfort zone, we are likely to organize our ignorance into lists and summaries that do not require further attention.

As I thought about the professor and "the assurance that this experience is unique" and about Jesus's capacity or specific transformative interaction, I thought as well afresh about the ministry of the church. Of course I am committed to the role of the church as an advocate for social justice. It is important, however, to remember that this advocacy is not a social-scientific enterprise in which we simply summarize. It is rather an advocacy that is based on the deep conviction that every one of our neighbors counts in his/her irascible individuality and specificity. We do indeed need to generalize for the sake of policy formation, but such policy formation is for the sake of individual persons whom we see in all of their individuality. For that reason, the life of a congregation should be flooded with stories about individual persons who have names, even while we care about justice in the large terms of race, gender, class, and ethnic origin. We may *generalize* only after we have *individualized*. And after we have *individualized* with specificity, we can again *generalize* for the sake of policy.

There can hardly be any doubt that the quintessential specificity of congregational life is in the sacrament of baptism wherein we perform, again and again, the mystery and the wonder of each person raised in grace and in celebration into the presence of God. In that moment when the celebrant says, "Name this child," or some such formula for an adult, something both specific and cosmic happens in a dramatic instant. We become known in that moment within the community and in the neighborhood. But we are also known by the angels in the most remote regions of God's heaven. With such a name, we are never again reduced to a generic tree but rather, as we say, we are "marked as God's own forever." We may imagine that Peter, at Pentecost, asked three thousand times, "Name this child, name this adult." Peter surely never wearied of the specificity!

So imagine the church, when it can muster its best liturgical courage, can say, "Name this child, Name this adult":

- Name this child who died in the Bronx because there was no fire escape.
- Name this adult who got caught in the madness of the insurgency of January 6.

- Name this child who was forced to go to a segregated, inadequate school.
- Name this adult massacred by missiles and tanks, under whatever flag.
- Name this child who organized book reading supplies for underfinanced children.
- Name this Swiss adult who provided hospitality for Romanian migrants fleeing north.

It is for this reason that we get the long genealogies in the Bible . . . every name counts! Thus we know the names of those who "came up out of captivity" (Nehemiah 7:6–65). We know the names of those who stood with Ezra and interpreted the Torah (8:7). We know the names of those who signed the covenant with Nehemiah (10:1–26). We know the names of the priests and Levites who came up from exile (12:1–16). We even know the names of those ordained to be deacons in the earliest church (Acts 6:5). In our rush we tend to skip over the names. In faith, however, we pause to name, and to recognize every one of them. We do not read in a hurry; we do not summarize or reduce to a sketch. Nor does the Holy One (Revelation 20:12)!

As the professor well knew, it is quite possible to dumb down and not read or learn anything more about the awesome variety of human experience. And then we are sure to make our own particular experience the norm whereby all others are measured. As Jesus knew, as long as we do not see at all, or only see "people walking like trees," we surely misperceive the wonder, depth, and particularity of God's creation in its manifold creatureliness.

A congregation might be a keeper of names, and a seer of individual persons. Such a community might regularly engage in a recital of names . . . of those in the news this week, of those who have contributed mightily to our common wellbeing, and those who have suffered the most in our common injustice. Such a congregation is a preserver of *human worth*, an enhancer of *human dignity*, and a custodian of *human possibility*. And all the while the world of power and wealth, of greed and fear rushes by with summaries and statistics, not delayed or impacted by the granular truth of another, different life. The names keep coming; we may stop and notice, a primal act in the formation of a functioning life-giving neighborhood.

4

STAY SAFE?

A LOCAL LUTHERAN church in our town has this on its street sign:

> *Love God*
> > *Love Your Neighbor*
> > > *Stay Safe.*

The first two imperatives, of course, are the primary commandments of Moses (Leviticus 19:18; Deuteronomy 6:5) and of Jesus (Mark 12:28–34). The third imperative that occurs nowhere in Moses or Jesus is with reference to the risks and dangers of the COVID-19 virus. They are all there together on the church sign. I have been shocked by the unambiguous contradiction between the first two and the third mandate. Concerning the third mandate, all of us want to be as safe as we can be. That is why we use masks, get vaccinated, and social distance. Clearly, however, neither Moses nor Jesus bid his followers to focus on such safety. Exactly the opposite. Consider:

> *You shall love the Lord your God with all your heart, and with all your soul, and with all your might.* (Deuteronomy 6:5)

The Bible is filled with accounts of those who set out to love God in full ways. It is that mandate that caused Abraham to leave his homeland, that caused Moses to confront Pharaoh, and that caused the prophets to address kings with mighty warnings and great threats. The champion obedient risk-taker in the New Testament has to be Paul:

> *I am talking like a madman—I am a better one: with*
> *far greater labors, far more imprisonments, with countless*
> *floggings, and often near death. Five times I have received*
> *from Jews the forty lashes minus one. Three times I was*
> *beaten with rods. Once I received a stoning. Three times I*
> *was shipwrecked, for a night and a day I was adrift at sea;*
> *on frequent journeys, in danger from rivers, danger from*
> *bandits, danger from my own people, danger from Gentiles,*
> *danger in the city, danger in the wilderness, danger at sea,*
> *danger from false brothers and sisters; in toil and hardship,*
> *through many a sleepless night, hungry and thirsty, often*
> *without food, cold and naked.* (II Corinthians 11:23–27)

Safely, anyone? Indeed we have a catalogue of those who "by faith" acted out the mandate of Moses.

> *All of these died in faith without having received the*
> *promises, but from a distance they saw and greeted them.*
> *They confessed that they were strangers and foreigners on the*
> *earth, for people who speak in this way make clear that they*
> *are seeking a homeland. . . . Therefore God is not ashamed to*
> *be called their God; indeed, he has prepared a city for them.*
> (Hebrews 11:13–16)

It is that same mandate that has evoked brave, risky behavior over the centuries in the church.

Indeed the saints are those who have not "stayed safe." While we have such dramatic cases of heroic actions, some of that same obedience is local and risk-running, even if it is mostly not heroic. At a recent dinner party in our local church among those present were three older couples. One couple had adopted a disabled child who had been abandoned. Another couple has initiated and sustained a regular program of care and food for disadvantaged people, a program that continues to feed about a hundred people in our town every day. A third couple has devoted much of their retirement to gardening that provides food for the food program. None of these couples has "played safe" with their time or energy or resources. They have been about obedience to that first commandment. They would not have undertaken these ventures if they had been playing safe.

In like manner, the imperative to love your neighbor is not a directive to stay safe. Of course the mandate is not to love our neighbor when it is convenient or safe. It is to love your neighbor as you love your own self, in every season and in every circumstance. That mandate has indeed caused obedient people to act out the very agenda of the Son of Man when he comes in his glory. You know the agenda:

> *I was hungry and you gave me food, I was thirsty and*
> *you gave me something to drink, I was a stranger and you*
> *welcomed me, I was naked and you gave me clothing, I was*
> *sick and you took care of me, I was in prison and you visited*
> *me.* (Matthew 25:35–36)

These are not zones of safety. Rather, they are areas of life that are disordered and disadvantaged, and subject to violence, deception, and exploitation. But that is where neighbors are to be found. And when it is not hands-on contact, it may be policy formation to the same end; or it may be contribution of monetary resources to sustain such actions and policies. Neighboring that has substance and staying power is not a safety pageant.

It turns out that those who take these two commandments seriously are not and cannot stay safe. That of course does not mean we should court danger for the sake of danger, but only in order to be obedient to these commands. It is wise, then, to recognize that this third mandate of the church sign is of a different ilk. It is not definitional for our faith in the way that the first two commands are. It belongs to a different universe of discourse. The problem with the church sign is that it does not and cannot distinguish between two very different universes of discourse. The first two imperatives are elemental and constitutive for the life of faith. The third is only an awareness that we should, in our obedience, be as "wise as serpents" (Matthew 10:16) about the risks we run in obedience to God and neighbor. The reality for many of us is that we are so wise and calculating that we never run the risk of real obedience or enter vigorously into the zone of neighborliness. Given that reality, it is a time in the church to think about how to be "innocent as doves," naïve about the possibilities of faith in the world. The church is not and will not be sustained by those who "stay safe." It is and will be sustained by those who embrace the first two commands and risk safety for the sake of God and neighbor. No doubt the roster of faithful people in our tradition is a procession of those who did not stay safe, who had more in common with doves than with serpents. Risks must be run, generosity must be performed, forgiveness must be enacted, and hospitality must be embraced. None of these is playing safe. There is no doubt that this is what Moses and Jesus had in mind. They never mentioned safety. Maybe we should add a clarifying footnote to the church sign at the Lutheran Church, in order to distinguish between real commandments and our knee-jerk caution.

❧ 5 ❧

THERE ARE CONSPIRACIES AND THEN THERE ARE CONSPIRACIES

WE HAVE BECOME inured to the Trump party and its readiness to find "conspiracy" at every level of opposition. Thus lawyers Rudy Giuliani and Sydney Powell eagerly identify conspiracy wherever there is opposition. They readily assume that there are hidden and secret powers lurking around voting machines seeking to overthrow the legitimacy of Trump's governance, whether it may be "the deep state," interference from Venezuela, or "Jewish money" clustered in Hollywood.

I was thinking about these eager illusionary accusations when I began to read *The Age of Reform* by Richard Hofstadter, the great historian at Columbia University. The book concerns the "progressive" political movement in the United States from 1890 through the New Deal. Writing in 1955 (at the peak of McCarthyism), Hofstadter wrote:

> *At the so-called grass roots of American politics there is a wide and pervasive tendency to believe—I hasten to add that the majority of Americans do not habitually succumb to this tendency—that there is some great but essentially very simple struggle going on, at the heart of which lies some single conspiratorial force, whether it be the force represented by the "gold bugs," the Catholic Church, big business, corrupt politicians, the liquor interests and the saloons, or the Communist Party, and that this evil is something that must be not merely limited, checked, and controlled, but rather extirpated root and branch at the earliest possible moment.* (16–17)

Hofstadter offers this as a recurring theme that marks the political life of the United States. And now the Trump regime thrives on such a notion. I suppose the positing of a conspiracy is a way to deal with (explain!) the forces that prove too powerful to manage or control among those who appeal to "conspiracy." It is certain that such a charge of "conspiracy" serves to draw attention away from the actual realities of socioeconomic political life.

Given that current Trumpian propensity and the more general analysis of Hofstadter, I decided to consider "conspiracy" in the Bible, that is, the secret plotting to overthrow established governance. In the political memory of ancient Israel, there are numerous charges of conspiracy. I have decided to focus on three usages of the notion of conspiracy.

First we may recognize that there are numerous reported actions of disruptions in the royal period, most particularly in the Northern Kingdom that lacked any legitimated dynasty. Thus Baasha versus Nadab (I Kings 15:27), Zimri versus Asa (I Kings 16:9), Omri versus Zimri (I Kings 16:16), the servants versus Joash (II Kings 12:20), the people versus Amaziah (II Kings 14:19), and Hoshea versus Pekah (II Kings 15:30). The only instance of conspiracy in Judah to the south was the people against Amnon and his short unhappy reign (II Kings 21:23–24).

Of all of these challenges to established governance, the most extended and interesting crisis is the case of Jehu against Joram. The narrative takes its time in reporting the actual killing of the king by Jehu (II Kings 9:14–26). And even in the report, the killing itself is portrayed as a settling of scores concerning the earlier action of the Omri dynasty (Ahab and Jezebel) against Naboth:

> *Lift him out, and throw him on the plot of ground belonging*
> *to Naboth the Jezreelite; for remember, when you and I rode*
> *side by side behind his father Ahab how the Lord uttered*
> *this oracle against him: "For the blood of Naboth and for*

> *the blood of his children that I saw yesterday, says the Lord,*
> *I swear I will repay you on this very plot of ground." Now*
> *therefore lift him out and throw him on the plot of ground,*
> *in accordance with the word of the Lord.* (II Kings 9:25–26)

The killing is justified because the regime was heterodox in its religious practices (v. 22), and because Naboth must be avenged.

Beyond the narrative itself, however, the conspiracy to overthrow the dynasty of Omri (Joash), we are told in the preceding that Jehu acted at the behest of the prophet Elisha who anointed Jehu to overthrow the regime:

> *Thus says the Lord the God of Israel: I anoint you king over*
> *the people of the Lord, over Israel. You shall strike down the*
> *house of your master Ahab, so that I may avenge on Jezebel*
> *the blood of my servants the prophets, and the blood of all*
> *the servants of the Lord. For the whole house of Ahab shall*
> *perish; I will cut off from Ahab every male, bond or free,*
> *in Israel. I will make the house of Ahab like the house of*
> *Jeroboam son of Nebat, and like the house of Baasha son of*
> *Ahijah. The dogs shall eat Jezebel in the territory of Jezreel,*
> *and no one shall bury her.* (II Kings 9:6–10)

The overthrow is thus said to be prophetically authorized. In his response to the killing of the king, moreover, Jehu gladly and openly claims legitimacy for his action:

> *It is I who conspired against my master and killed him.*
> (II Kings 10:9)

This is a remarkable narrative without parallel in the Old Testament that marks a major disruption of established governance in northern Israel. The dynasty of Omri, we know, had been remarkably successful in trade and military power. But according to the religious fanatics gathered around Elisha, that success and prosperity were ill-founded and untenable for serious Yahwists. Thus, according to the narrative, the conspiracy that ended the dynasty was done in the name of and at the behest of YHWH and his prophet. But then, I suppose that every serious conspiracy claims high ground, if not theological, then at least political or historical. Remarkably, John Calvin can end his Institutes with this final verdict:

> *But in the obedience which we have shown to be due to the authority of governors, it is always necessary to make one exception, and that is entitled to our first attention, that it do not seduce us from obedience to him, to whose will the desires of all kings ought to be subject, to whose decrees all their commands ought to yield, to whose majesty all their sceptres ought to submit.* (*Institutes of Christian Religion* [n.d.], Book IV, chapter XX, 804–5)

Calvin then quotes Acts 5:29:

> *We ought to obey God rather than men.*

And then he concludes:

> *Christ has redeemed us at the immense price which our redemption cost him, that we may not be submissive to the corrupt desires of men, much less be slaves to their impiety.* (805–6)

Of course it is a very long way from Jehu, Elisha, and Naboth to Geneva. Nonetheless the testimony is consistent. There is a place for such "conspiracy" against governance that is, in the end, illegitimate and to be rejected. The narrative of II Kings 9–10 that concludes with a bloodbath of the entire royal family (II Kings 10:1–10), occupies a central place in Israel's royal memory. It is a merciless narrative that attests to the tricky insoluble interface of faith and power, of governance and loyalty. Thus the "conspiracy" of Jehu is treated by the narrator as different in kind from the many upstart conspiracies that had no such prophetic grounding. But since the prophetic grounding for Jehu's action happened in private, this "legitimate conspiracy" looks from the outset like all the others. In the report YHWH is said to be a destabilizing force.

Two other uses of "conspiracy" in the Old Testament may claim our attention. In Jeremiah 11:1–13, in the cadences of the tradition of Deuteronomy, the prophet articulates Israel's failure in covenant with YHWH. The prophet first reiterates the reality of the covenant (vv. 1–6). But then he asserts that the people have broken the covenant and have brought big trouble on themselves:

> *Yet they did not obey or incline their ear, but everyone walked*
> *in the stubbornness of an evil will. So I brought on them all*
> *the words of this covenant, which I commanded them to do,*
> *but they did not.* (v. 8)

That single verse voices both the *verdict* and the *consequence* of broken covenant. But then, in what follows, the matter is further explicated. The violation of covenant with YHWH is said to be a "conspiracy" against the legitimated rule of YHWH, a rule legitimated by the covenant oaths stated above. The conspiracy against YHWH is delineated:

> *Conspiracy exists among the people of Judah and inhabitants*
> *of Jerusalem. They have turned back to the iniquities of their*
> *ancestors of old, who refused to heed my words; they have*
> *gone after other gods to serve them; the house of Israel and the*
> *house of Judah have broken the covenant that I made with*
> *their ancestors.* (vv. 9–10)

The consequence of their disobedience is a great "disaster." Thus the prophet utilizes the political imagery of "conspiracy" in order to delineate the theological infraction that has immense consequences. It is as though there were a "secret plot" to abrogate the rule of YHWH. This is a quite astonishing use of the notion of conspiracy.

The other prophetic usage that has drawn my attention is the dramatic encounter of the prophet Amos and the priest, Amaziah, at the royal shrine in Bethel (Amos 7:10–17). The narrative begins with the priest's dramatic charge against the prophet:

> *Amos has conspired against you* [the king] *in the very center of the house of Israel; the land is not able to bear all his words. For thus Amos has said,*
> > *Jeroboam shall die by the sword,*
> > *and Israel must go into exile away from his land.* (v. 11)

Amaziah proposes that Amos has secretly plotted to overthrow the legitimated governance of Jeroboam. (It is to be noted that Jeroboam II belongs to the dynasty of Jehu mentioned above. So quickly has that new dynasty initiated by Jehu come to success and prosperity, and hostility from the voices of critical Yahwism!) The great-grandson of Jehu is now under prophetic indictment. In fact, however, Amaziah's charge misrepresents the words of Amos. He charges that Amos threatened the person of the king. In verse 9, however, Amos has spoken of a "sword against the house of Jeroboam," not against the person of the king. But in mounting a charge of conspiracy against Amos, the priest does not quibble with such detail. It is enough, for the royal priest, to dispose of Amos as a dangerous, unwelcome, and illicit voice. The defensiveness of the royal house and its priest easily portray Yahwistic truth-telling as conspiracy against legitimated governance. It is easy enough for prophetic truth-telling to be dismissed as treasonable utterance. In the same way Jehoiakim would later shred prophetic words, as though by shredding them he could silence prophetic truth-telling (Jeremiah 26:23).

It is evident that the notion of conspiracy can be turned in various directions, as the actual overthrow of legitimated governance (II Kings 9–10), as theological indictment for the rejection of the rule of YHWH (Jeremiah 11), or for the dismissal of prophetic truth-telling (Amos 7). Given the plasticity of the term, it is no wonder that Hofstadter can use it to describe the near paranoia that continues to recur in US political rhetoric. It is enough, in our own contemporary moment, for those who are dissatisfied and made unhappy by the newly emerging multiracial culture, to entertain convenient notions of conspiracy in order to cope with emerging social reality which they cannot manage, control, or even understand. As the crisis of our democracy grows ever more acute, we may anticipate more such talk of ominous, unidentified forces that threaten the vanishing status quo.

My thought is that the truth-telling vocation of the church is to attest the claim of the gospel as a means by which to adjudicate every claim of conspiracy. The norms of the gospel are not complex or obscure, even if they are difficult. It is first to *love God*, to trace out the truth of God that consists in "justice, righteousness, compassion, steadfast love and faithfulness" (see Hosea 2:19–20). This characterization of God belongs to none of our preferred ideologies or idolatries. Thus the church is not called to be progressive or radical, liberal or conservative, but only to tell the truth about God who will not be contained in any of our favorite pettiness. It is, second, to *love neighbor*—the widow, the orphan, the immigrant—all those who lack advocate or resource. Such attestation of *love of God* and *love of neighbor* stands over against our every conspiracy to overthrow the rule of God by idolatry or by ideology (see Jeremiah 11), and against every false charge of conspiracy against prophetic truth-telling (see Amos 7). The enterprise of *love God* and *love neighbor* can and must be extended toward the public processes of our society. When we do so, we are able to "follow the money" and to see where and how and in what ways money weighs in order to skew truth-telling. It belongs to the truth-telling work of the church to sort out the ways in which money can be easily confused with wisdom, virtue, or legitimacy. Hofstadter concludes his reflection on conspiracy with these words:

> *It is widely assumed that some technique can be found that will really do this* [extirpate root and branch], *though there is always likely to be a good deal of argument as to what that technique is.* (17)

When the matter is closely considered, however, no special technique is required. All that is required is *love of neighbor* that goes with *love of God*. All the rest is distraction. The church is no party to special techniques. It has only that mandate that pertains in every circumstance. As I write this, Donald Trump Jr. is reported to have said to a Turning Point USA crowd on December 19 that Jesus's mandate to "turn the other cheek" has "gotten us nothing." Just so! The work of the church is "to get us nothing," but to bear witness to the kind of life that permits neighborly wellbeing. That claim is as old as the Deuteronomic work of Jeremiah. It is as simple and straightforward as the utterance of Amos at Bethel. It continues to be the truth entrusted to us—not complex, not hidden, and not conspiratorial.

❦ 6 ❧

WHO KNOWS?

THE HEBREW BIBLE has a recurring grammatical usage in response to the realities of life that are hidden, uncertain, filled with wonder, or beyond human comprehension. The repeated response to such uncertainty is, "Who knows?" (*mi-yodea'*):

> *While the child was still alive, I fasted and wept; for I said,*
>   *"Who knows? The Lord may be gracious to me, and the*
>   *child may live."* (II Samuel 12:22)

> Who knows *whether he will not turn and relent,*
> *and leave a blessing behind him,*
> *a grain offering and a drink offering for the Lord, our God?*
>   (Joel 2:14)

> Who knows? *God may relent and change his mind; he may turn*
>   *from his fierce anger, so that we do not perish.* (Jonah 3:9)

> Who considers *the power of your anger?*
> *Your wrath is as great as the fear that is due you.* (Psalm 90:11)

> *My child, fear the Lord and the king,*
> *and do not disobey either of them;*
> *for disaster comes from them suddenly,*
> *and* who knows *the ruin that both can bring?* (Proverbs 24:22)

> Who knows? *Perhaps you have come to royal dignity for just*
>   *such a time as this.* (Esther 4:14)

The intent is to assert either that *only God knows* and is not telling, or *no one knows*. Either way, human persons are left without knowing.

But of course the human quest for certitude is unquenchable and wants, however possible, to overcome such "unknowing." That quest for certitude may take the form of science (even though good science always opens up new doors of the unknown), or the form of religious certitude (even though such claims are never fully disinterested). In the end, however, all such quests are defeated by the hidden dimensions of reality that do not readily open up for us.

The human community, nonetheless, arrives at certitude as best it can, overcoming the "not known." It is habitual, and surely evident in Western culture, that "knowing" is a top-down practice, wherein those with more learning, or more power, or more wealth claim to know, and often have their claims accepted as reliable and trustworthy. We may term this common assumption and ready practice an "epistemology of privilege." Those privileged know the best. As a result, when we get the open-ended question, "Who knows?" We readily respond:

> The doctor knows best.
> The teacher knows best.
> The banker knows best.
> Father (or mother) knows best.

And of course one cannot gainsay that there are areas of competence and expertise that are essential and to be valued, competence and expertise as in the roles of a brain surgeon, a pastor, an airline pilot, or a therapist. Beyond such competence or expertise, however, there is a common readiness to assign "gifts of knowing" to those on the top side of social power. As a result, we easily and unthinkingly extend the claim on order to assume:

> *Whites know better than people of color;*
> *Men know better than women;*

Colonialists know better than "natives":
Tenured teachers know better than other teachers;
Entrenched political leaders know better than protesting
*   students;*
Police know better than protesting marchers.
Capital knows better than labor.
Abled people know better than the disabled.

While these claims are evidently sometimes true, the important point is
that this advantage in knowing is widely and readily assumed in every case,
without reference to the particulars. It is assumed, moreover, by both those
who claim such advantage and by those who submit to such advantage.

As I was writing this, I was reading *Albion's Seed: Four British*
Folkways in America by David Hackett Fischer (1989). Fischer studies
four different waves of British migration to America, from four
different regions of Britain to four different regions in America. One
of the American regions is the gentile society of Virginia about which
Fischer writes:

> *Just as the gentlemen of Virginia deferred to their King, so*
> *the yeomanry were expected to defer to gentlemen, servants*
> *were required to submit themselves to their yeoman masters,*
> *and African slaves were compelled to submit themselves to*
> *Europeans of every social rank. These rules were generally*
> *obeyed in Virginia. . . . Deference also had a reciprocal*
> *posture called condescension. . . . For its* [Virginia's ruling
> elite] *social purposes, it required an underclass that would*
> *remain firmly fixed in its condition of subordination. The*
> *culture of the English countryside could not be reproduced*
> *in the New World without this rural proletariat. In*
> *short, slavery in Virginia had a cultural imperative. . . .*
> *Hierarchical violence of this sort was commonplace in*
> *Virginia.* (385, 388, 403)

I cite this material as a clear, unambiguous, extreme example of the "epistemology of privilege."

The claim I wish to exposit here is the notion that the testimony of the Bible is essentially a *revolution in epistemology* that challenges the top-down assumption of an epistemology of privilege. My academic friend, Brian Walsh, speaks of "the epistemological priority of suffering." That is, those who have suffered know some dimensions of reality better than those who have not suffered and who therefore have no access to those dimensions of reality. This "revolution in knowing" suggests the upending of much conventional authority and the recognition of authority in places and by persons we have little suspected of having authority.

The epistemological revolution performed in the Bible is rooted in nothing less than the character of YHWH, an active agent surely "on top," but willing, able, and ready to live life "from below" along with those who receive from YHWH special attention and advocacy. That revolution from "an epistemology of privilege" to "an epistemology of suffering" is dramatically articulated at the outset of the Exodus narrative. In response to the cries and groans of enslaved Israel, YHWH responds:

> *God heard their groaning, and God remembered his covenant*
> *with Abraham, Isaac, and Jacob; God looked upon the*
> *Israelites, and God took notice of them. . . . Then the Lord*
> *said, "I have observed the misery of my people who are in*
> *Egypt; I have heard their cry on account of their taskmasters.*
> *Indeed, I know their sufferings, and I have come down to*
> *deliver them from the Egyptians. . . ."* (Exodus 2:24–25,
> 3:7–8)

In that moment of attentive response, YHWH "sees, hears, knows, and comes down." From that moment YHWH is allied with and present with those who occupy the slave camps. The stretch of that epistemological conversion is voiced in the doxology of Deuteronomy 10:17–18:

> *For the Lord our God is God of gods and Lord of lords, the*
> *great God, mighty and awesome, who is not partial and*
> *takes no bribes, who executes justice for the orphan and the*
> *widow, and who loves the strangers, providing them food and*
> *clothing.*

YHWH indeed on top of the heap of the gods! But without a pause, this wondrous sovereign power is resituated in verse 18. Now YHWH is engaged in justice work alongside widows, orphans, and immigrants, the core occupants of "below." Instead of doxological wonder that the gods might indeed enjoy, this God is engaged with food and clothing, the quotidian stuff upon which the hazardous lives of widows, orphans, and immigrants depend. From that moment of "descent," the narrative of YHWH concerns the truth of suffering and the newness that arises in and through and amid suffering.

Given this resituating of divine presence within the slave community, the drama that follows is sure to surprise. In the unequal context between the learned "magicians" of Pharaoh, with all of their technological advantage and the efforts of Moses and Aaron on behalf of the slave community, we might expect that the advanced capacity of Pharaoh would prevail. But of course the narrative is told and remembered precisely because such a routine expectation of "top-down" capacity does not prevail. Thus by the third episode in the contest, Moses and Aaron produced gnats. And then we are told:

> *The magicians tried to produce gnats by their secret arts, but*
> they could not. (Exodus 8:18)

Surprise! *They could not!* Imagine! Top-down authority and learning could not match the competence of the slave leaders; they could not match such power because YHWH had allied YHWH's own life with the slave community that had become the freighted locus of divine power and divine presence. Thus Moses is celebrated as a spectacular embodiment of the "epistemology of suffering." Moses knows about suffering! In the process of his suffering, moreover, he has come to a capacity to enact great wonders that exposed Pharaoh's top-down authority as a fraud. It does not surprise us that in what follows Moses becomes the voice and performer of the new epistemology that gives access to the will, power, and presence of the emancipatory God. That remarkable access of course is unavailable to top-down Pharaoh who is left with only his impotent idols of power and wealth.

The "epistemology of suffering" set in motion by YHWH and made visible and effective by Moses and Aaron continues as the theme of the faith of Israel. The prophets continue that epistemology from below as they practice truth speaking to power. We may say that such a prophetic trajectory comes to its fullest expression in the remarkable assertion of Jeremiah in his assault on the royal person and policy of Jehoiakim. Speaking of Josiah, the father of Jehoiakim, Jeremiah has God say:

> *Did not your father eat and drink*
> *and do justice and righteousness?*
> *Then it was well with him.*
> *He judged the cause of the poor and needy;*
> *Then it was well with him.*
> *Is not this to know me? Says the Lord.* (Jeremiah 22:15–16)

Knowledge of God is offered in, with, and under *justice for the vulnerable*. It is not different in the wisdom tradition as it is asserted that,

> The fear of the Lord *is the beginning of knowledge;*
> *fools despise wisdom and instruction.* (Proverbs 1:7)

> *Truly,* the fear of the Lord, *that is wisdom;*
> *and to depart from evil is understanding.* (Job 28:28)

> *The end of the matter: all has been heard.* Fear God *and keep*
> *his commandments; for that is the whole duty of everyone.*
> (Ecclesiastes 12:13)

Attentiveness to YHWH, the emancipator of slaves, is the locus of true knowledge! Thus both the prophets and the wisdom teachers in sum agree in recognizing the epistemological breakthrough that has been dramatically performed by Moses and Aaron. All of these trajectories have little patience with an epistemology of privilege and doubt its effectiveness or validity.

It is not a surprise to notice that Jesus stands in this Israelite tradition of wisdom from below. On the one hand, when he made his appearance in the synagogue in Nazareth, he astounded those who heard him:

> *On the sabbath day he began to teach in the synagogue, and*
> *many who heard him were astounded. They said, "Where did*
> *this man get all this? What is this wisdom that has been given*
> *to him? What deeds of power are being done by his hands! Is*
> *not this the carpenter, the son of Mary and brother of James*
> *and Joses and Judas and Simon, and are not his sisters here*
> *with us?"* (Mark 6:2–3)

His wisdom was recognized, even though he was from the village and the son of a carpenter. It was not anticipated that such a man, a young man, would be so wise. But Jesus knows! On the other hand, his prayer of thanksgiving in the tradition of Matthew asserts that "these hidden things" are entrusted to babies:

> *I thank you, Father, Lord of heaven and earth, because you*
> *have hidden these things from the wise and the intelligent*
> *and have revealed them to infants.* (Matthew 11:25)

Such wisdom is withheld from those who are supposed to know . . . the wise, the learned, the intelligent, and the authoritative. In this singular utterance Jesus manifests the epistemological revolution that was his life's work. These verses illuminate the special welcome Jesus offers to children to whom the Kingdom of God belongs (Mark 10:14), for the little children possess none of the "knowledge of the world" but engage in a different way of knowing marked by innocence and trust.

But of course it is the crucifixion of Jesus at the hands of Rome that is the extreme suffering of the life of Jesus. Thus the cross, as the vehicle of his execution, became the symbol of obedient suffering that pertains to Jesus (see Philippians 2:8) and to his followers (see Mark 8:34, 10:21). Beyond that reality of the suffering of Jesus, in Trinitarian theology the cross is also the marker of the suffering of God. Thus Jürgen Moltmann can conclude:

> *To recognize God in the cross of Christ, conversely, means to recognize the cross, inextricable suffering, death, and hopeless rejection in God.* (*The Crucified God* [1974], 277)

Thus Jesus is the embodiment of the suffering love of God that confounds the wisdom of the world. It is from that reality of Jesus that the followers of Jesus bear and perform the knowledge of God rooted in suffering, and contradicts the world by its capacity for self-giving.

This *epistemological revolution* from *an epistemology of privilege* to *an epistemology of suffering* is the key work of the church. *What* we know is shaped by *how* we know. Every time the church meets it is again to acknowledge and perform this epistemological revolution, to make clear to ourselves (and to others!) that our ways of knowing and recognizing the truth are shaped in and through suffering. From this it follows that the church is an arena where the suffering of the world receives attention, not only in the big sweep of world issues, but close at hand concerning the bearers of suffering who are everywhere present in the neighborhood.

Thus we may return to the question posed by Mordecai to Esther:

*Who knows? Perhaps you have come to royal dignity for just
such a time as this?* (Esther 4:14)

Who knows? Who indeed knows about just such a time as this? Who
knows what the moment requires? The tradition is clear enough. Those
who know are those who have participated in the suffering of the world
and who therefore bear a kind of power that contradicts the normal
power of the world. When the church gathers, it meets to acknowledge
this peculiar, inexplicable power and to mobilize that power yet again
for a different life in the world.

In his exposition of the life of Simone Weil, Robert Zaretsky
(*The Subversive Simone Weil: A Life in Five Ideas* [2021]) reports a
conversation that Simone de Beauvoir sought out with Simone Weil.
Weil had given her life away in solidarity with French workers. When
Beauvoir asked her about her remarkable work, Weil tersely dismissed
Beauvoir, concluding that because she had not suffered she could not
understand. So it is with *knowing and suffering*. When we have not
participated in the suffering of the world, we do not and cannot understand. The narrative of the church concerns the suffering love of God,
belatedly embodied in Jesus that has now been peculiarly entrusted
to the church. We live and act and think differently because we know
differently.

⤳ 7 ⤳

WITHOUT HINDRANCE!

ON A RECENT windy day Tia and I went to our beautiful West Bay in Traverse City in order to see the waves. The waves were four or five feet high, splashing over piers and cars. There were, nonetheless, ducks floating serenely upon the waves, bobbing up and down with the waves, seemingly completely unbothered and without vexation. It occurred to me that the ducks were without hindrance, not hindered by waves or by wind or by readily floating debris.

Seeing the ducks float "without hindrance" caused me to remember a final verdict on the apostle Paul in the last verse of the book of Acts. The writer (Luke) reports that Paul was in Rome,

> *Proclaiming the kingdom of God and teaching about the*
> *Lord Jesus Christ with all boldness and without hindrance.*
> (Acts 28:31)

Given what we know about Paul and his many "toils and snares," it is reassuring (and surprising!) that in his later days he could continue his bold work "without hindrance," not hindered by imperial authorities in Rome where he proclaimed "another kingdom." Nor was he hindered by Gentiles who baited him or by Jews who contested with him (see Acts 17:16–21). I could imagine Paul, not unlike those ducks, floating serenely about his work, unhindered, unbothered, and undisturbed.

This is a remarkable verdict on Paul, given what we know of his vexed life and ministry. He himself summarizes the many hindrances that he faced:

I am talking like a madman—I am a better one: with
far greater labors, far more imprisonments, with countless
floggings, and often near death. Five times I have received
from the Jews the forty lashes minus one. Three times I was
beaten with rods. Once I received a stoning. Three times I
was shipwrecked; for a night and a day I was adrift at sea;
on frequent journeys, in danger from rivers, danger from
bandits, danger from my own people, danger from Gentiles,
danger in the city, danger in the wilderness, danger at sea,
danger from false brothers and sisters; in toil and hardship,
through many a sleepless night, hungry and thirsty, often
without food, cold and naked. And, besides other things, I
am under daily pressure because of my anxiety for all the
churches. (II Corinthians 11:23–28)

All of that, however, seems to have been processed and digested (not forgotten!) in ways that permit Paul to finish "without hindrance."

This collection of "hindrances" that accumulated for Paul over time is likely more hazardous than most preachers face. But every preacher, in a moment of self-pity not unlike that of Paul, could as well offer a recital something like that of Paul. It might go like this:

I feel—when I think about it—like a madman (or mad
woman). Countless insults, often near humiliation that has
filled me with lingering hurt. I have received from believing
folk forty hostile phone calls minus one. Three times I was
harshly critiqued unfairly by my board. Once I had my
monthly check withheld by a stubborn treasurer. Two times I
have had folk cancel their pledges in anger. For a night and
a day I knew myself to be abandoned and without support,
danger from my own congregation, danger from outsiders in
the community, danger from neighbors, danger from fickle

colleagues, danger from a remote unsupportive judicatory . . .
many a sleepless night . . . under daily pressure because of
anxiety for the church.

None of this is as heroic as is Paul. It is, nonetheless, enough to cause sleepless nights and vexed days, with loss of appetite, temptation to drink . . . weak . . . made to stumble, and indignant (see II Corinthians 11:29). Nobody said being a preacher would be easy. So how could Paul then be "without hindrance"? How could ducks float in a storm without hindrance? How could contemporary preachers continue in boldness in ministry without hindrance? Luke, in the book of Acts, does not tell us, but he certainly knew of Paul's inventory of vexations.

We are free to imagine Paul as a child of the gospel who so fully trusted in God's faithfulness that all his tribulations were kept in manageable perspective. He does not deny them, or disregard them, or minimize them. He names them and looks them full in the face. Indeed, perhaps he treasures them as his markers of his boldness and fidelity. He nonetheless submits all of his troubles to the deeper, more elemental, more reliable claim of the gospel. He not only *proclaims* the goodness of God; he himself *entrusts his own life* to that goodness. This permits Paul, in his later years but surely all along the way, to turn his attention and energy away from his every trouble to the deep truth of the gospel that he has embraced. Indeed we may imagine that the ducks float serenely through the storm because they know that the water would hold. The water is trustworthy and buoyant, and will not fail because of the wind.

Thus I imagine a local pastor, much beset in the congregation:

Arguments about the color of the chancel carpet, disputes
about the schedule of the youth program that collides
with a basketball game, feuding families that preclude
congregational harmony, irate parishioners who flail at

*a critiques of "45" or "being too political," even if done
obliquely.*

The local preacher can be done in by such daily challenges from those
who are trapped in various alienations. The local preacher alternatively
can, like the ducks, trust the buoyancy of the water, be like Paul to fall
back into the goodness of God in a way that makes all the tribulations
distinctly penultimate. To refocus attention on the basics is not easy
in the midst of a troubled day. But no doubt those who embrace the
freedom of the gospel are able to see past *the daily storm* to the *abiding
buoyancy.*

I am not sure the ducks are singing when they quack. But if they
are singing, I hope they have in their repertoire this hymn that I sang
in my growing up years:

*Jesus, Savior, pilot me
Over life's tempestuous sea;
Unknown waves before me roll,
Hiding rock and treach'rous shoal.
Chart and compass came from thee;
Jesus, Savior, pilot me.*

*As a mother stills her child,
Thou canst hush the ocean wild;
Boist'rous waves obey thy will
When thou say'st to them, "Be still!"
Wondrous Sov'reign of the sea,
Jesus, Savior, pilot me.*

*When at last I near the shore,
And the fearful breakers roar
'Twixt me and the peaceful rest,
Then, while leaning on thy breast,*

May I hear thee say to me,
"Fear not; I will pilot thee."

This was a hymn for Paul in his many days of trouble. It is a hymn for preachers every day. We do not need to be on automatic pilot; nor do we need to be at sea rudderless. Imagine differently the voice of the One who sees the waves and says in sovereign calmness, "Be still." It is enough to live with "without hindrance."

Part II

SOCIAL PAIN AND POSSIBILITY!

❧ 8 ❧

HABEAS CORPUS

FROM MY EARLIEST days I learned in church to recite the creed. In my tradition it was the Apostles Creed. I learned to recite it before I had any clue about the meaning of the words or phrases. I learned and loved the cadences of the creed, and felt solidarity with all those who made the same recital, who were no doubt also without many clues about its meaning. Of course the creed finishes with the strong affirmation of the work of the Holy Spirit who is free to violate all of our categories of explanation:

> *I believe in the Holy Spirit,*
> *the holy catholic church,*
> *the forgiveness of sins,*
> *the resurrection of the body,*
> *and the life everlasting. Amen.*

Except that in our vigilant anti-catholicism we refused to say the word "catholic" even in lower case, and instead said, "the one holy universal Christian Church," our cumbersome euphemism for the word, "catholic." And of course it is not different in the Nicene Creed that I learned to recite and love in my adult Episcopal years. The ending of the creed is different and perhaps more carefully nuanced, but much the same in essentials:

> *We believe in the Holy Spirit, the Lord, the giver of life,*
> *Who proceeds from the Father and the Son.*
> *With the Father and the Son he is worshiped and glorified.*

He has spoken through the prophets.
We believe in one holy catholic and apostolic church.
We acknowledge one baptism for the forgiveness of sins.
We look for the resurrection of the dead,
   and the life of the world to come. Amen.

The phrasing is somewhat different, perhaps a tad softer with "the resurrection of the dead" that we may take as synonymous with "the resurrection of the body." This usage, in both creeds, relies on the apostolic testimony concerning the resurrection of Jesus that is taken as an earnest and guarantee for our more general expectation of resurrection. From the outset the church has insisted on the resurrection of Jesus from which it has extrapolated a more general evangelical hope of resurrection of our bodies.

The church believes and trusts that we are elementally bodies, and that God cares for and provides for our bodily existence and well-being. This insistence is neatly and succinctly voiced in Genesis 2:7 where it is affirmed:

Then the Lord God formed man from the dust of the ground,
and breathed into his nostrils the breath of life; and the man
became a living being.

That is, we are bodies that have been breathed on, and when the breath that we cannot control is taken from us, our bodies are dust with the hope of being breathed on yet again. This claim intends to combat and counter the popular claim that we are embodied (incarnated) spirits, and when our spirit leaves the body at death, our spirits continue to live elsewhere and otherwise. The "resurrection of the body" intends to oppose and resist any notion of the "immortality of the soul," the easier claim of much generic religion. After all, if our souls were "immortal," there would be no need for God, whereas "resurrection of the body" recognizes and affirms that in death, as in life, we are wholly dependent upon the generous, life-giving attentiveness of the creator God. The claim of "resurrection" of the body of course poses immense problems, as is evident in Paul's thick, not-very-clear explication of the claim:

> *So it is with the resurrection of the dead.*
>
>> *What is sown is perishable, what is raised is imperishable.*
>> *It is sown in dishonor, it is raised in glory.*
>> *It is sown in weakness, it is raised in power.*
>
> *It is sown a physical body, it is raised a spiritual body. If there is a physical body, there is also a spiritual body. Thus it is written, "The first man, Adam, became a living being"; the last Adam became a life-giving spirit. But it is not the spiritual that is first, but the physical, and then the spiritual. The first man was from the earth, a man of dust; the second man is from heaven. As was the man of dust, so are those who are of the dust; and as is the man of heaven so are those who are of the heaven. Just as we have borne the image of the man of dust, we will also bear the image of the man of heaven.*
> (I Corinthians 15:42–49)

Biblical faith, in both Jewish and Christian articulation, is insistent on the claim of "the body."

To be sure, there are mixed and unclear testimonies in the gospel narratives about the "resurrection appearances" of Jesus, and our own continuing interpretive perplexity about the "bodily" claim is evident in the text and in the tradition. Beyond that, moreover, we are willy-nilly heirs of Descartes and his dualism that could argue that reality is wondrously "mind" that need not linger over the inconveniences of "matter." And behind the legacy of Cartesianism, among others, is the wise judgment of Socrates:

> *Only the body and its desires cause war, civil discord and battles, for all wars are due to the desire to acquire wealth, and it is the body and the care of it, to which we*

> *are enslaved, which compels us to acquire wealth, and all*
> *that makes us too busy to practice philosophy.* (quoted by
> Norman Wirzba, *This Sacred Life: Humanity's Place in a*
> *Wounded World* [2021], 40)

Indeed Wirzba traces out with some precision the contemporary "transhuman urge," the quest for escape from the requirements of our "bodily existence" into a "better place" without bodily inconveniences (*This Sacred Life*, 34–60). Wirzba avers that Google, through its company, Calico, is actively working "to solve death" (45). All of this effort by the very wealthy is a continuation of the very old notion of "immortality" that wants to be free of the impediments of bodily existence. Such a free-floating imagination in the interest of wellbeing to perpetuity fails to reckon with the reality that such ease, comfort, and convenience will continue, elsewhere as here, to depend upon cheap labor implemented by bodies that will grow tired and old.

Given that old, long-running, and contemporary yearning to have a body-free existence, it is worth pausing to recognize that the biblical tradition is steadfastly and uncompromisingly insistent concerning the bodily reality of our historical existence. Problematic as it is, the claim is beyond doubt so that the church stands against all such escapist inclinations, fully affirming our bodily existence. We are creatures whose lives are bodily shaped and bodily destined because we are bodies—flaws, warts, and all. As bodily creatures, we rely upon the provision ("providence"!) the creator God makes for us. The point is made clearly and simply in the catechism:

> *God constantly proves himself to be the Creator by his fatherly*
> *providence, whereby he preserves and governs all things . . .*
> *God daily and abundantly provides for me with all the*
> *necessaries of life, protects and preserves me from all danger . . .*
> *God does all this out of sheer fatherly and divine goodness*

and mercy, without any merit or worthiness on my part. (The
Evangelical Catechism, 19–20)

This defining and unaccommodating claim of gospel faith has
been freshly and poignantly made for me in a remarkable op-ed piece
by Esau McCaulley, "What Good Friday and Easter Mean for Black
Americans" (*New York Times*, April 17, 2022). McCaulley affirms the
"resurrection of the body":

> *Christians believe that our bodies will be resurrected from the*
> *dead to live in this transformed earth. Like the earth itself,*
> *these bodies will be transfigured or perfected, but they will*
> *still be our bodies.*

But then he offers a painful survey of the African American bodily
existence in the United States from "the auction block to the lynching
tree, to the knee on the neck of George Floyd." The long painful
history of African Americans in our country is the history of white
control over Black bodies, control that was and continues to be readily
violent and brutal. He cites the final display of the maimed body of
Emmitt Till (as ordered by his mother) as an exhibit of Black bodies
"lynched, maimed and martyred" as a reminder of the "high cost of
Black freedom."

That is why, as McCaulley makes clear, "the resurrection of the
body" is so crucial for faith and for public life. He affirms that Jesus
was raised "with his brown, Middle Eastern, Jewish body." And then
he makes this affirmation:

> *When my body is raised, it will be a Black body. One that*
> *is honored alongside bodies of every hue and color. The*
> *resurrection of Black bodies will be the definitive rejection of*
> *all forms of racism. At the end of the Christian story, I am*
> *not saved from my Blackness. It is rendered everlasting. Our*

bodies, liberated and transformed but still Black, will be the
eternal testimony of our worth.

He lays down the challenge of faith:

The question, "What will God do about the disinherited and
ripped apart bodies of the world?" can be seen as the central
question of religion. Either give me a bodily resurrection or
God must step aside. He is of no use to us.

It is the case that the more "intellectually sophisticated" we are,
the more "the resurrection of the body" is problematic, as it violates
our Enlightenment rationality. It is the case, in equal manner, that the
more affluent we are, the more money we can and will spend on bodily
comfort, ease, and convenience that we readily take as a right. The
less "intellectually sophisticated" we are, the more we are left with the
uncompromising reality of our bodily existence, and the less affluent
we are, the less we can afford the care of our bodies in ways that lead to
comfort, wellbeing, and safety. Thus our intellectual sophistication and
our affluence together may talk us out of our bodily reality. But those
who are less sophisticated and less affluent are left with their bodies
and the pain that willy-nilly comes with our bodies.

Thus the centrality of the body for gospel faith is elemental and
nonnegotiable. We can and no doubt will continue to engage in speculation about the risen body of Jesus, a reality that violates our best
reason. But we do better to use our energy, political will, and intellectual insight in valuing more fully our own bodies and the bodies of all
of our neighbors. Our conventional practice in our racist society is to
regard Black bodies as a resource for our convenience that are otherwise
quite dispensable. To the contrary, our gospel faith requires that public
resources must be mobilized in generous ways for the care and wellbeing of all of our bodies that includes the *bodies* of young vulnerable
children, the *bodies* of disabled people, the *bodies* of women, the *bodies*

of old people, and the *bodies* of people of color, the *bodies* of those with alternative gender identity, all those *bodies* that fall outside the horizon of care of white male hegemony. It is of course an exemplary scandal that too many fierce "pro-life" advocates are deeply resistant to government finance for the care and nurture of bodies once they have been brought to life. It is as though too many "pro-life" advocates propose to abandon the lives of babies when they have insisted that they be brought to life. This readiness to abandon is part of a larger readiness in our society to devalue the bodies of all of those who do not qualify in the ruling hegemony.

There is no way, finally, to separate our confession of "the resurrection of the body" from good public policy that aims to nurture, guard, protect, maintain, and enhance the wellbeing of every human body among us. Our creedal confession leads us in a direct way to the mobilization of policies and funds for care and protection of the vulnerable. It is telling that Paul, in his great ethical summons, urges that we "present our bodies as a living sacrifice" (Romans 12:2). Paul goes on, in that wondrous chapter, to delineate the faithful practices of properly dispatched bodies in the work of solidarity, generosity, and hospitality. And in his exposition of the resurrection in I Corinthians 15, he ends with the ethical commendation:

> *Therefore, my beloved, be steadfast, immovable, always*
> *excelling in the work of the Lord, because you know that in*
> *the Lord your labor is not in vain.* (I Corinthians 15:58)

The "work of the Lord" from the outset has concerned the rehabilitation of the vulnerable (see Luke 7:22). It is the "work of the Lord" to be engaged in concrete, specific, and public ways in the work of resurrection.

The writing of Norman Wirzba, moreover, has shown how "care for the body" is deeply linked to care for the environment, for the environment is the creator's way of providing a viable habitat for all the creatures. There is no escaping this habitat, so it must be cared for. As for those who seek or hope to escape to a "better place," Wirzba nicely concludes:

> *The focus and goal of our efforts, in other words, should not be to seek* transportation *to another world, but the* transformation *of the desires and habits that are rendering our only world uninhabitable.* (44)

It is time, I judge, that the church can and must call the bluff on all those who denigrate the body, who neglect the positive capacity of the body politic, and who willfully foul the environment in ways that make our shared bodily existence increasingly risky and in jeopardy.

9

LET US NOW PRAISE FAMOUS
HEALTH-CARE PROVIDERS

THE APOCRYPHA OF the Old Testament includes the book of *Ecclesiasticus, The Wisdom of Jesus Son of Ben Sirach.* The book, a collection of various kinds of wisdom sayings, is commonly dated to 180 BCE. In what follows I will juxtapose two famous sections of the book as background for my appreciation of caregivers.

First, in Ben Sirach 38 there is a celebrative ode concerning doctors (38:1–15):

> ***Honor physicians*** *for their services,*
> *for the Lord created them;*
> *for their gift of healing comes from the Most High,*
> *and they are rewarded by the king.*
> *The skill of physicians makes them distinguished,*
> *and in the presence of the great they are admired.*
> *The Lord created medicines out of the earth,*
> *and the sensible will not despise them.* (vv. 1–4; emphasis
>   added)

Lest there be any tension between *faith* and *medical science*, the writer sees that medicine is a good gift from the creator God. As direct advice for the sick, the writer urges prayer, penitence, and offerings to God:

> *My child, when you are ill, do not delay,*
> *but pray to the Lord, and he will heal you.*
> *Give up your faults and direct your hands rightly,*

> *and cleanse your heart from all sin.*
> *Offer a sweet-smelling sacrifice, and a memorial portion of*
>   *choice flour,*
> *and pour oil on your offering, as much as you can afford.*
>   (vv. 9–11)

But after these urgings of piety, room is made for the doctor:

> *Then give the physician his place, for the Lord created him;*
> *do not let him leave you, for you need him.*
> *There may come a time when recovery lies in the hands of the*
>   *physicians,*
> *for they pray to the Lord*
> *that he grant them success in diagnosis and in healing,*
> *for the sake of preserving life.* (vv. 12–14)

The final aphorism links sin against the creator God to defiance of the doctor:

> *He who sins against his maker,*
> *will be defiant toward the physician.* (v. 15)

This linkage of God and doctors is not unlike Proverbs 17:5 that voices a direct link between mocking the poor and insulting the creator. As the poor are intimately linked to God, so doctors are closely connected to the creator.

The other citation from Ben Sirach to which I make appeal here is the long section of 44:1–50:21 introduced by the familiar phrase, **"Let Us Now Praise Famous Men."** What follows is a long list of "famous men" in the memory of Israel who are indeed as men of faith who contributed effectively to the life of Israel. (Yes, the list includes only men, even though the tradition markedly includes many women of faith who mattered decisively, including Sarah, Miriam, Deborah,

Hannah, and Hulda.) In this rendition the writer names men of prominence, but then acknowledges that there are many others not included or remembered:

> *But of others there is no memory;*
> *they have perished as though they had never existed;*
> *they have become as though they had never been born,*
> *they and their children after them.*
> *But these also were godly men,*
> *whose righteous deeds have not been forgotten;*
> *their wealth will remain with their descendants,*
> *and their inheritance with their children's children.*
> *Their descendants stand by the covenants;*
> *their children also, for their sake.*
> *Their offspring will continue forever,*
> *and their glory will never be blotted out.* (44:9–13)

There is some irony in this acknowledgment since the writer intends to identify "famous men." This juxtaposition suggests that some who are *not famous* are indeed to be honored alongside the famous.

The move from "famous men" (in our case "famous doctors") to those most often not mentioned or remembered permits us to recognize and take with serious appreciation those health-care deliverers who are most often not mentioned or remembered. Our move in this same direction is helped along by the classic book of James Agee and Walker Evans, *Let Us Now Praise Famous Men* (1941). Agee and Walker take up the well-known introductory phrase of Ben Sirach 44:1 in order to present a study of three sharecropper tenant farmers and their families in Alabama. Their names are Fred Garvrin Ricketts, Thomas Gallatin Woods, and George Gudger. The prose of Agee and the photography of Walker present what they can see and observe, almost without interpretive comment. Nor do they comment on the title they have used, even though its usage is thick with irony. The point of the title, I take it, is that these sharecropper farmers and families are not "famous," but they are worthy of close and appreciative attention. So it is with our consideration of health-care deliverers. Many of them are not "famous," but they are worthy of appreciative attention.

The long recital of "famous men" in Ben Sirach 44–50 includes, at the outset, Enoch and Noah, and then the patriarchs of Genesis; then follow the names of historical narrative memory including kings (David, Solomon, Rehoboam, Jeroboam, Hezekiah, and Josiah), but alongside the kings are the prophets, Elijah, Elisha, and Isaiah. The list concludes with reference to "Simon," a Maccabee, from nearer the writer's own time (50:1–21). All of these "famous men" are grounded in faith; they did bold things for their people.

My thought here is to link chapter 38 on doctors and chapters 44–50 on "famous men" so that we may especially consider famous doctors (along with many other health-care providers who, even though it is as if "they had never been born," will have their names recalled in generation after generation). They are the doctors, nurses, and medical technicians not widely known, but to whom specific persons and families are abidingly grateful for the careful, caring work they have done.

Now as I juxtapose *doctors* and *famous men*, I want to reflect on the life and work of Paul Farmer who has just died (see "He Wanted to Make the Whole World His Patient" by Tracy Kidder, *New York Times*, February 22, 2022, A20). Farmer was the Presley Professor of Medical Anthropology at Harvard Medical School. With that as his home base, Farmer moved around the world into the deepest trouble spots, mobilized his medical skills, his great compassion, and his alert social imagination to transform societies and countries into healing venues. Especially in Rwanda and notably and abidingly in Haiti, Farmer put his buckets down to impact the lives of many needy and desperate people. His work is described in the biography by Tracy Kidder, *Mountains beyond Mountains: The Quest of Dr. Paul Farmer, a Man Who Would Cure the World* (2003) and in Farmer's own book, *Pathologies of Power: Health, Human Rights, and the New War on the Poor* (2005).

Farmer brought to his work a keen awareness of the force of rapacious power, the ways in which power apportioned health resources, and ways in which symbol systems make for inclusive or exclusive care. He was powerfully informed by liberation theology, discerning the ways in which social injustice impinged upon health care:

> *But we will critique them* [social democracies], *and bitterly, because access to the fruits of science and medicine should not be determined by passports, but rather by need. The "health care for all" movement in the United States will never be morally robust until it truly means "all."* (*Pathologies of Power*, 152–53)

He understood that truth about social reality is not monopolized by those with power and money:

> *Truth—and liberation theology, in contrast to much postmodern attitudinizing, believes in historical accuracy—is to be found in the perspective of those who suffer unjust privation. Cornel West argues that "the condition of truth is to allow the suffering to speak. It doesn't mean that those who suffer have a monopoly on truth, but it means that the condition of truth to emerge must be in tune with those who are undergoing social misery—socially induced forms of suffering."* (153)

In his appeal to liberation theology, he saw that "charity medicine" is often "second-hand, cast-off service." To the contrary he insisted:

> *The notion of a preferential option for the poor challenges us by reframing the motto: the homeless poor are* more *deserving of good medical care than the rest of us. Whenever medicine seeks to reserve its finest services for the destitute sick, you can be sure it is option-for-the-poor medicine.* (155)

Following the work of George Pixley and Clodovis Boff, Farmer critiqued developmental approaches to health-care delivery that are based on "liberal" views of poverty:

> *Liberal views place the problem with the poor themselves;*
> *these people are backward and reject the technological fruits*
> *of modernity. With assistance from others, they too will, after*
> *a while, reach a high level of development. Thus does the*
> *victim-blaming noted in the earlier discussion of tuberculosis*
> *recur in discussions of underdevelopment.* (155)

Farmer's deep understanding of the matter of health-care delivery as it is related to liberal values (and violence!) was matched by his personal attentive compassion and generosity. Kidder, in "He Wanted to Make the Whole World His Patient," described one moment in Farmer's engagement with his patients:

> *Paul was visiting a hospital to meet with Peruvian doctors*
> *about a different patient when he ran into the boy's mother*
> *and father and saw the boy running toward him down*
> *a hospital hallway, actually* running. *The boy wasn't just*
> *healed, he was restored. After cries of delight and hugs,*
> *Paul met with the Peruvian doctors and then headed to*
> *the parking lot. I sensed that someone was following us. I*
> *turned, and so did Paul, and we saw the little boy's mother*
> *with her head bowed. She came up to Paul and said in*
> *Spanish, "I want to say many thanks." Paul immediately*
> *took her hands and said also in Spanish, "For me, it is a*
> *privilege."*

The wonder of Farmer's work is that he combined the patient attentiveness of a real live doctor with his acute awareness of how social structures and social policies impinge on the health or unhealth of the "undeserving" people with whom he used his skills. He is indeed a "famous man" who should be praised, remembered, and celebrated.

From his extraordinary life two things occur to me while you, dear reader, may think of many others. First, while Farmer is and was "larger than life," he may be a stand-in for the countless doctors, nurses, and health-care providers who do the daily hard work of medicine, who possess technical competence and human passion, and who give themselves away in tireless work in hard circumstances and against great odds. Many of them will leave no memory and will be "as though they have never existed." Except that in the midst of our forgetfulness, their names will "never be blotted out" because some grateful family will recall them and their brave, tireless work. Thus, for example, my Dad from his younger days always remembered "old Doctor Bunge" in Bland, Missouri. He never spoke of him other than as "old Doctor Bunge" who had saved his life in an emergency appendectomy and who eventually mentored him to seminary and into ministry. My Dad's life was better because of "old Doctor Bunge." And his name lingers for us!

Second, it is possible and important to read our present health-care crisis in our society through the lens of Farmer's work. While we quibble variously about coverage, co-pays, deductions, and drug prices—all made as complicated as possible—the simple obvious daily reality of our society, matched by our affluent resources, is a travesty and an embarrassment. Our economic circumstance does not require parsimony toward those who need health care. Rather, our circumstance might regularly evoke open-handed generosity that is capable of health care for all those who require it. Of course the bugaboo is "socialism," a term that is reiterated as often as possible. But that of course is a phony quarrel. What is not phony is the way in which generous resources are withheld from the common good, and the way in which the powerful ration care for the vulnerable.

It belongs exactly to the work of the church to educate about the common good, and the allotment of common resources for the sake of the common good. It is exactly the capitalist ideology of extreme individualism that makes our parsimony toward the poor, needy, and vulnerable seem like a virtue. If we require a text to make thecrisis clear, we might consider the juxtaposition of Acts 4:32–37 and 5:12–11. In the former, the clear mandate is that the community held "all things in common." In the latter, Ananias and Sapphire are rebuked (and dead!) precisely because they withheld property and profit from the community.

> *Yes, let us praise famous men and women!*
> *Yes, let us praise famous doctors, nurses, and all other health-*
> *   care providers.*
> *Yes, let us praise those who are most often mentioned and whose*
> *   names are not remembered at all:*

> *Then give the physician his place, for the Lord created*
> *   him;*
> *do not let him leave you, for you need him.* (Ben Sirach
>   38:12)

And then let us resolve to do the hard work of learning from Dr. Farmer that good medical practice requires a restored decision for communal solidarity. It might be a good idea to take up Farmer's own book, *Pathologies of Power*, as a study guide for the congregation. After all, what Famer knew and practiced is simply the core obligation of our faith. It is no wonder that when Jesus sent out the seventy, he gave them a simple terse charge:

> Cure the sick *who are there and say to them,* "The Kingdom
>   of God *has come near to you.*" (Luke 10:9)

The coming Kingdom is the practice of neighborliness, the redistribution of resources, the valuing of the most vulnerable, and the rehabilitation of the most hopeless. Ben Sirach declares:

There may come a time when recovery lies in the hands of
physicians,
for they too pray to the Lord that he grant them success in
diagnosis and in healing,
for the sake of preserving life. (38:13–14)

The withholding of good health care is indeed a way to defy the doctor. It is also a way to sin against our Maker:

He who sins against his maker,
will be defiant toward the physician. (38:15)

Jesus reiterates after he commissions the healers:

Yet know this: the kingdom of God has come near! (Luke 10:11)

10

NOT COMFORTED!

WE HAVE JUST seen the film, *Philomena*. It is a story of "Philomena," the title character (played by Judi Dench), who as a young Irish girl had a baby. Because of her shaming pregnancy, she was sent to a convent where she lived with the stress of harsh disapproval and hard (Magdalene-like) labor in a laundry. In what is said to be based on a true story, her little baby, Martin, whom she treasured dearly, was sold for adoption to a wealthy US couple who took him away from the convent in a fancy car. The film consists in Philomena's desperate, urgent determination (fifty years later) to find her son, Martin. Led and supported by Martin Sixsmith, who is a reporter (played by Steve Coogan), she eventually is able to trace her son to Washington DC where he had become an important Republican operative. At the outset Sixsmith was only looking for a good story; he was, nonetheless, slowly won over to share her urgent quest. Finally she finds Martin's gay partner, only to learn that Martin has died of AIDS. But she also learns that Martin's partner had thoughtfully and generously taken his body and laid it to rest in the graveyard of the Irish convent where she had birthed him. Only with assurance of the belated "homecoming" of Martin, as she visits his grave, does Philomena find some solace.

The film, as might be expected, led me to a trajectory of biblical texts that concern lost children. At the outset I thought of Joseph in the book of Genesis. Joseph was the belated son of Jacob, spoiled by his father and despised by his older brothers. His brothers, in their resentment against him, resolved to kill him. They were, however, restrained by their oldest brother, Reuben (Genesis 37:21–22). Another older brother, Judah, has a better idea with a chance for economic gain. He proposes that the brothers "sell" Joseph for a "profit" (vv. 26–27). Thus

Joseph, not unlike Martin, turns out to be a profitable commodity. The brothers, not unlike the Irish nuns, make money by the sale of a child, in this case, for "twenty pieces of silver" (v. 28). We are not told how much money the nuns received for Martin.

Their father, Jacob, is not unlike mother Philomena. When Jacob sees the evidence of the staged murder of his son, he is disconsolate:

> *He recognized it, and said, "It is my son's robe! A wild*
> *animal has devoured him; Joseph is without a doubt torn to*
> *pieces." Then Jacob tore his garments and put sackcloth on his*
> *loins, and mourned for his son many days.* (vv. 33–34)

His sons play their expected social role, seeking to comfort their father. Jacob's daughters, who were not in on the plot, also try to comfort their desolate father. But then, we are told:

> *He refused to be comforted, and said, "No, I shall go down to*
> *Sheol to my son, mourning." (v. 35)*

Jacob would not be comforted. He could not be comforted. In that moment Jacob relives the anguish and the grief that has beset this chain of fathers and sons in the book of Genesis. Thus Abraham, when he is summoned to offer up his son:

> *Take your son, your only son Isaac, whom you love, and go to*
> *the land of Moriah, and offer him there as a burnt offering*
> *on one of the mountains that I shall show you.* (Genesis 22:2)

Father Isaac, when he learned of the ruse of Jacob to secure a blessing that was not his:

> *Then Isaac trembled violently and said, "Who was it then*
> *that hunted game and brought it to me, and I ate it all before*
> *you came, and I have blessed him?"* (27:33)

And son Esau matched the violent response of his father:

> *He cried out with an exceedingly great and bitter cry, and*
> *said to his father, "Bless me, me also, father!"* (v. 35)

But the grief of Jacob is deeper and more severe than that left unexpressed by Abraham, or the disruption of Isaac, or the pathos of Esau. He could not be comforted. When the brothers proposed to take beloved young Benjamin with them to Egypt, father Jacob must reiterate and reperform his most durable grief:

> *My son shall not go down with you, for his brother is dead,*
> *and he alone is left. If harm should come to him on the*
> *journey that you are to make, you would bring down my gray*
> *hairs with sorrow to Sheol.* (42:38)

Only late in the narrative, after the cunning disposal of Joseph and the careful protection of Benjamin, only then do the brothers return from Egypt in order that they may report to their father:

> *Joseph is alive! He is even the ruler over all the land of Egypt.*
> (v. 26)

Jacob's response does not surprise us:

> *He was stunned; he could not believe them. But when they*
> *told him all the words of Joseph that he had said to them, and*
> *when he saw the wagons that Joseph had sent to carry him,*
> *the spirit of their father Jacob revived. Israel said, "Enough!*
> *My son Joseph is still alive. I must go and see him before I*
> *die."* (vv. 26–28)

He was stunned! The Hebrew says "His heart overturned." Indeed, his life was overturned as he was at long last comforted. No doubt Jacob would have said, had he known the words of the later father rendered in parable:

> *This son of mine was dead and is alive again; he was lost and is found.* (Luke 15:24)

Jacob finds a better comfort than did Philomena; "My son is alive and well!"

But of course the tradition is not finished with this final comfort of Jacob. The prophet Jeremiah, so long after the stories of the ancestors, can remember that dreadful scene of the grief over Joseph. Only now the prophet, in his acute sensibility, can transfer the grief from *father Jacob* to *mother Rachel.* Beyond the Genesis narrative, mother Rachel is scarcely mentioned in the Bible (see only Ruth 11:4). But Jeremiah's stressful time required him to dig into the pain of the tradition. He knows, moreover, that he can go no deeper into the pain of the tradition than the memory of Jacob's pain concerning Joseph. So the prophet listens! What he hears is lament and bitter weeping. He knows it is "weeping and bitter lament" over Jerusalem that is about to be sacked, over the temple that is about to be razed, and over Israel that is about to be exiled. And he knows the accent of the weeping. It is the sound of mother Rachel. In the Genesis story Rachel is written out of the account of Joseph's would-be death. But now she is restored as the mother of deep grief:

> *Thus says the Lord:*
> *A voice is heard in Ramah, lamentation and bitter weeping.*
> *Rachel is weeping for her children; she refuses to be comforted*
> *for her children,*
> *because they are no more.* (Jeremiah 31:15)

She refuses to be comforted! She is exactly like her husband Jacob in the Genesis narrative who also refused to be comforted. Rachel, not unlike Jacob, is also not unlike Philomena. All of them have lost a child. All of them grieve.

The story of grief, in all of these cases, is very deep. But it is not beyond reach. Jacob is comforted when he readies to go see his son in Egypt. Philomena is comforted when she finds that Martin is at rest in his grave, when he had come home to her. As for mother Rachel, in her grief, the prophet speaks a word of comfort to her:

> *Thus says the Lord:*
> *Keep your voice from weeping,*
> *and your eyes from tears;*
> *for there is a reward for your work, says the Lord;*
> *they shall come back from the land of the enemy;*
> *there is hope for your future, says the Lord;*
> *your children shall come back to their own country.* (vv. 16–17)

For Jeremiah, Rachel is weeping for the lost children of exile, sons and daughters, treasured and now deported. Jeremiah, however, knows more. He can and will anticipate a great homecoming worked by the God of all restoration. There is hope! There is this inscrutable expectation that Israel will come home because the God of the Genesis fathers and mothers is the God who keeps promises.

We might imagine that we have finished with Joseph, Jacob, Rachel, and their grief. Joseph has been found! In the narrative Rachel has been reassured by the prophet. Except that in the narrative account of Jesus by Matthew, Rachel in her grief is retrieved one more time in the only mention of mother Rachel in the New Testament. Now the reperformance of greedy violence against vulnerable children occurs yet again. It was greedy brothers that caused Joseph to be sold to merchants. It was greedy violence that caused Israel's displacement to Babylon. And now, via Matthew, it is the greedy violence of King Herod that leads to brutality against the children (Matthew 2:16–18). In order to stop the threat of the baby Jesus, Herod implements a massacre of the new children who are in the reach of his regime. In doing so, he reiterates the fearful violence of Pharaoh in Exodus 1:16. The action of Herod is recognized by Matthew to be a replay of old violence. If we listen as Matthew listened, as Jeremiah had listened, we can hear the weeping. If we have paid attention, we can identify that particular accent of the weeping. In the wake of the grief of father Jacob, this weeping is the inconsolable sobbing of mother Rachel yet again. With the assurance of the prophet Jeremiah, we might have thought that Rachel had finished weeping. Except in the world of greedy violence, mother Rachel is never finished weeping:

> *Then was fulfilled what had been spoken through the prophet Jeremiah;*
> *A voice was heard in Ramah, wailing and loud lament.*
> *Rachel weeping for her children;*
> *She refused to be consoled, because they are no more.* (Matthew 2:18)

She refused, one more time, to be comforted! She is as she was in the Jeremiah tradition. She is like her husband, Jacob, in the Genesis narrative who also refused to be comforted. Her tears would not be assuaged. She is like Philomena as long as she had not found Martin. All of them grieve. All of them have lost a child. Rachel is, as Emil Fackenheim has written, still weeping over six million lost and not recovered . . . just lost!

All of this comes into view with the film of Philomena. I had and have no need to make further connection beyond this triad of texts concerning Jacob and Rachel and their grief. Except that we are not finished with weeping over children, refusing to be comforted. It is too bad that the so-called "pro-life" movement is, for the most part, only a "pro-birth" movement, without a care for the ongoing life of the newly born children. So now we live in a culture where children live in poverty, food disadvantage, exposed to the violence that comes easily along with poverty and food deprivation.* Of course an effective response to such social failure requires complex policy decisions and deployment of adequate resources.

But such policies require social resolve. We have one such policy proposal in the "Build Back Better" offer of President Biden. That program would bring great relief to children through affordable child-care and preschool opportunity. There is plenty of room for negotiation on the specifics, and plenty of resources that can be allotted to such concerns. All that is needed is political will. All that is needed is an attentive focus on the actual children and the risks they face in poverty, hunger, and violence. Notice of children in poverty, hunger, and violence will and must evoke tears among us . . . tears of the *recognition* of suffering, tears of *penitence* for social failure, tears of *shame* for uncaring indifference and maybe—in the end—tears of *hope* for restoration, homecoming, and the assurance that these children can not only live but prosper. In my judgment it is the case that without tears of *recognition*, *repentance*, *shame*, and *hope*, there will be no resolve or energy for enactment of policy.

We should, in the face of social violence, refuse to be comforted. We refuse, until something is done. We refuse until children are noticed, treasured, and protected. We refuse until money is invested and programs are initiated. We refuse until all of our children are given the elemental resources for life and wellbeing. We live in the shadow of the God who is "father (and mother) of orphans" (and of other unprotected uncared for children) (Psalm 68:5). This God will refuse to be comforted until we learn the tears of effective alertness. Then, we shall be comforted,

> *comforted like Jacob,*
> *comforted like Rachel,*
> *comforted like Philomena.*

---

* See the wise, suggestive appeal to the name of mother Rachel by Jonathan Kozol, *Rachel and Her Children: Homeless Families in America* (1988).

Imagine: No more the sound of weeping! No more the cries of deso-
lation! No more violence toward the vulnerable. No more! Then our
deep nighttime tears may be turned to tears of joy:

> *Weeping may linger for the night,*
> *but joy comes in the morning.* (Psalm 30:5)

When we have done our homework we may then, with Paul, bless the
God of all comfort:

> *Blessed be the God and Father of our Lord Jesus Christ, the*
> *Father of mercies and the God of all consolation, who consoles*
> *us in all our affliction, so that we are able to console those*
> *who are in any affliction with the consolation with which we*
> *ourselves are consoled by God.* (II Corinthians 1:3–5)

SPEAK TRUTH; DO JUSTICE

FOR NO REASON beyond my curiosity I recently read a biography of John Charles McQuaid (*John Charles McQuaid; Ruler of Catholic Ireland* by John Cooney [1999]). McQuaid was the long-running Catholic archbishop of Dublin in the mid-twentieth century, before, during, and after Vatican II. With a strong authoritarian propensity, McQuaid took as his work the creation, maintenance, and protection of Ireland as a pure Catholic country. In order to accomplish this ambitious task, he sought to purge the public life of Ireland of all other influences—secular, modern, or Protestant. In his ruthlessness he was singularly adept at shaping public policy in which he frequently equated his own whim or inclination with the will of God. He regularly invoked the punishment and wrath of God on whatever behavior he disapproved. He was especially eager to protect his faith community (that he equated with civic society) from bad influences concerning sexuality. He was particularly attentive to the protection and wellbeing of the young boys in this regard. He played up to Rome in the most direct way in the hope of being made a cardinal, but he never was so appointed.

The single page in Cooney's book that most struck me was the list of books banned by the Catholic hierarchy of Ireland, a banning vigorously urged by McQuaid. According to Cooney, the list of banned authors included the following:

James Joyce, Sean O'Casey, Sigmund Freud, Maxim Gorky, Thomas Mann, Alberto Moravia, Graham Greene, H. G. Wells, George Bernard Shaw, Sean O. Faolain, Frank

O'Conner, Liam O'Flaherty, Kate O'Brien, Oliver St. John
Gogarty, Bertrand Russell, George Orwell, Noel Coward,
Christopher Isherwood, Aldous Huxley, Compton MacKenzie,
Sinclair Lewis, W. Somerset Maughan, Ernest Hemingway,
Taylor Caldwell, Upton Sinclair, Truman Capote, Henry
Morton Robinson, Robert Penn Warren, Sherwood Anderson,
William Faulkner, F. Scott Fitzgerald, Margaret Mead,
Martha Gellhorn, John Dos Passos, Joyce Carey, Marcel
Proust, Anatole France, Jean Paul Sartre, Andre Gide, and
Simone de Beauvoir. (242)

The list seems more or less random, until it is recognized that all of
these books, in various idioms, open up a world of daring imagination
of a modern secular kind to which the scholastic hierarchy in Ireland
was strongly opposed. The bishops obviously thought that the banning
of books would preclude the invasion of new ideas into the cultural
landscape of Ireland. And for a season, as long as their stern authority
prevailed, the banning was effective . . . for a season! The bishops
hoped to eliminate any interpretive venue that did not conform to
and enforce their narrow articulation of reality permitted by their rigid
scholastic faith.

Reading this page on the banning of books called to my mind one
of the most dramatic encounters in the Old Testament. In Jeremiah 36
it is reported that the prophet, Jeremiah, dictated a scroll to his scribe,
Baruch. That dictation, it is presumed, became the substance of our
book of Jeremiah. Because the prophet himself was *persona non grata* to
the king and so banned from the temple, he dispatched Baruch to read
the scroll in the temple (vv. 8–10). When the leadership of the king's
cabinet heard the words of the scroll, they questioned Baruch and he
read the scroll to them. The scroll, evidently, laid out *the wayward-*
ness of royal Israel that took the form of greedy exploitation against
the vulnerable poor. The scroll, moreover, indicated that such policies
and practices were sure to bring upon Israel *the sanctions of the ancient*

covenant of Sinai. It is no great wonder that the leadership was alarmed at such a prospect, and reported the matter to King Jehoiakim.

When the scroll was read aloud to King Jehoiakim, he very ostentatiously cut the scroll (shredding!) and tossed it into the fireplace. The king clearly assumed that if he disposed of the scroll, he would at the same time dispose of the social analysis and sanctions voiced in the scroll by burning the prophetic words. He assumed that burning the prophetic scroll would protect his realm from the hard, uncompromising truth of the prophet. Just to be on the safe side, the king organized a posse to seek out and arrest Jeremiah and Baruch. The text reports, laconically, "The Lord hid them" (v. 26). We are not told the means of such hiding, but we may imagine that some of the royal leadership recognized the legitimacy of the prophetic words, and so intervened to protect them (see 26:24). It strikes one that the work of the archbishop in banning the books and the work of the king in burning the scroll serve the same purpose. In both cases the intent is to protect and maintain the status quo by silencing voices to the contrary and to deny the categories of interpretation that disrupt the absolutism of present arrangements. Thus the banning and the burning are designed to maintain status quo without interference, and so to protect a social arrangement of privilege and advantage, even if that privilege and advantage are based on a misconstrual of social reality.

The banning by the archbishop and the burning by the king have been on my mind as we have heard reports of local governments and school boards banning the teaching of "Critical Race Theory." Those who fear and resist "Critical Race Theory" have taken the phrase and reified it into an ominous identifiable principle as a threat to the status quo. In fact the phrase "Critical Race Theory" is simply an ordered, disciplined way of studying the way in which racism and white supremacy have prevailed in and dominated US history. It is nothing more (or less) than the recovery of our national history that has been infused with racism. Thus while George Wills can declare that the advocates of "Critical Race Theory" want to teach our children to "hate

America," in truth they simply want our children to learn our past and to accept responsibility as heirs of that unhappy past.

The prohibition (banning, burning!) of the teaching of Critical Race Theory is not unlike the banning of books and the burning of the scroll. It is an effort to maintain a status-quo social arrangement of advantage, privilege, and domination; that maintenance requires a continuing, intentional ignorance of our real history. But what we learn, repeatedly, is that such banning, burning, and prohibition finally will not work. It will not work because the truth will out, even if it is sorry truth. Thus the banning of books in Ireland could last only as long as the Catholic bishops could maintain their outsized authority that was bound to be overthrown by the emancipating workings of the historical process. Thus while Jeremiah and Baruch were for a time slowed in their testimony, Jeremiah 36, in the end, reports that Jeremiah redictated the scroll, and Baruch rewrote the scroll, and so we have the book of Jeremiah. The narrative ends with the teasing terse conclusion, "Many similar words were added" (v. 32). The books finally could not be banned in Ireland. The scroll would not stay burned in Jerusalem. Indeed, in II Kings 22:11–13, in what many interpreters think is designed as a counterpoint to Jeremiah 36, King Josiah, the good king who was father of Jehoiakim, receives the scroll found in the temple, responds to its summons, and acts on its imperative. In the end, it is certain that the forces of denial and resistance will not stop the fresh telling of the racist past of our society. Such refusal and resistance will not silence the retelling of our past because there are many insistent advocates who will not be silenced. More than that, the resistance cannot prevail because truth will out in a world where the God of all truth presides. Soon or late, we will come to an awareness that the honest facing of our racist history is the only means whereby we can move beyond the fear that yields denial, the fear that produces anger—and eventually violence. The cover-up cannot succeed here anymore than it could in Dublin or in Jerusalem.

We have everywhere in my town a sprinkling of the same yard sign. That sign says, simply, "Speak truth, do justice." The sign appears in odd and unexpected places because here and there folk know what is required. The sign compellingly confirms that "truth" and "justice" go together; if there is no truth-telling, there will be no justice. Thus the archbishop sought to repress the truth, and that led to deep practices of injustice. Thus the king refused the truth of the scroll, and that was alongside the practice of exploitative injustice. It is reported in Jeremiah 22:13–14 that the king used unfair labor practices and prospered on cheap labor. In our own society, when we do not tell the truth of our long, vexed history of racism, we are sure to let the claims and practices of white supremacy go unnoticed and unchecked. Thus truth-telling must resist book banning and scroll burning. Even now, in our moment of truth-telling, the state of Texas has provided that no book can be used in school that may evoke "discomfort, guilt, or anguish." In the state of Pennsylvania, students have in some places rejected the practice of using only books that attest white privilege. And this just in from the *New York Times*, February 17, 2022: Marcus Dohle, the CEO of Penguin Random House, has donated $500,000 to PEN, a writers' group that resists book banning and that promotes freedom of publication. Dohle reported that his action was in a concern to protect free speech that is essential in a democracy.

It is certain that *speaking truth* is as urgent as *doing justice* for the church. It is my quite practical thought that, in venues where teaching "Critical Race Theory" is banned, the church may have an obligation to engage in just such teaching in order to overcome such aggressive denial. Just as the scroll of Jeremiah had "many similar words added," so our work is to add many similar words that may contribute to our "discomfort, guilt, and anguish," but is a *sine qua non* to our emancipation and to the wellbeing of our democracy. We might better respond to the painful truth-telling of books in the way that father Josiah did, unlike his son, Jehoiakim:

> *Did not your father eat and drink*
> *and do justice and righteousness?*

Then it was well with him.
He judged the cause of the poor and needy;
then it was well.
Is not this to know me? Says the Lord. (Jeremiah 22:15–16)

Josiah knew that such *truth-telling* alongside *justice-doing* is the prerequisite of wellbeing. It is so in Dublin, in Jerusalem, and among us. It will not and cannot be otherwise.

STRANGE BUSINESS!

HERE IS A new word you may not know, "schismogenesis," that taken literally means "originated in a split." It was coined in 1935 by Gregory Bates ("Cultural Contact and Schismogenesis," *Man* 35 [1935]: 178–83). I learned it by reading *The Dawn of Everything: A New History of Humanity* by David Graeber and David Wengrow (2021). These authors, following Bates, characterize the term in these words:

> Bateson coined the term *"schismogenesis"* to describe people's tendency to define themselves against one another. Imagine two people getting into an argument about some minor political disagreement but, after an hour, ending up taking positions so intransigent that they find themselves on completely opposite sides of some ideological divide—even taking extreme positions they would never embrace under ordinary circumstances. . . . People come to define themselves against their neighbors. Urbanites thus become more urban, as barbarians become more barbarous. . . . They will all definitely exaggerate their differences in arguing with one another. . . . Each society performs a mirror image of the other. In doing so, it becomes an indispensable alter ego, the necessary and ever-present example of what one should never wish to be. (56–57, 180)

In speaking of Indigenous peoples on America's West Coast they write:

> The more the uplanders came to organize their artistic and ceremonial lives around the theme of predatory male violence,

*the more lowlanders tended to organize theirs around female
knowledge and symbolism—and vice versa.* (245)

We can observe this same tendency in our society as we seek
to delineate "good Americans" in contrast to immigrants, gays, or
Muslims. In an exaggerated form we can see it in the readiness of people
to relocate in order to be in a "Red" or "Blue" social context. The
tendency is well advanced in our society as differences are sharply exaggerated in order to make distinctions. None of this is more poignant in
our society than the fact that vaccines and masks have become totems
for tribal identity. Thus in "Masks: Angry Up in Northern Michigan,"
Ron French (*Record-Eagle*, March 7, 2022) reports on a meeting in
Traverse City in which adversaries about masks and vaccines lined up
on opposite sides of the room and screamed at each other. The participants in this destructive interaction likely did not know they were
performing Bateson's "schismogenesis"!

The same propensity to *difference through exaggeration* is operative
in the Old Testament, as is evidenced in the "purity codes" of the Torah;
see, for example, Leviticus 11:1–47, Deuteronomy 14:3–21. The intent
is to distinguish a "holy" people from all other peoples. In Deuteronomy
23:1–8, the list of the excluded, stated with forceful vigor, pertains to
those with crushed testicles (perhaps those who accommodated imperial
powers by becoming eunuchs, on which see Isaiah 56:3–5), bastards,
and the Moabites and the Ammonites. In the first two instances, no
reason for exclusion is given; perhaps it was assumed the reason was
evident in social shame. But concerning Moabites and Ammonites, the
reason for exclusion is a quite particular narrative memory. Curiously, at
the end of the list of exclusions, exceptions are made for the Edomites
and the Egyptians who may be admitted if they are the third generation.
Everywhere the point is to protect the identity and preeminence of the
hosting people, an identity and preeminence assured by the exclusion
of the others. It does not take much of an extension of this reasoning to
establish supremacy and superiority of a "holy" kind.

In the face of Bateson's telling term and its fear-filled operation among us, I have been thinking about the remarkable declaration in Deuteronomy 10:17–19 (notice that it is this same book of Deuteronomy that hosts the purity code of 14:3–21 and the list of exclusions in 23:1–8):

> *For the Lord our God is God of gods and Lord of lords, the great God, mighty and awesome, who is not partial and takes no bribes, who executes justice for the orphan and the widow, and who loves the strangers, providing them food and clothing. You shall also love the stranger, for you were strangers in the land of Egypt.* (Deuteronomy 10:17–19)

In this quite remarkable text we have an extraordinary doxology concerning YHWH. YHWH is praised and celebrated as "God of gods" and "Lord of lords" who presides over the divine council. But then abruptly amid verse 17, the exclamation moves from *theological affirmation* to quite particular *economic matters*, no bribes that could only be paid by the wealthy, sustenance for the widows and orphans (those without male advocates in a patriarchal society), and love of strangers, that is, embrace of those "unlike us." That "love of strangers," moreover, is quite quotidian and practical, concerning food and clothing.

This statement traces the movement of YHWH from the realm of the gods to the sphere of welfare for needy human persons. One can see in the Christian tradition, how this "descent" of God from the heavenly to the earthly sphere is performed in the life of Jesus "who emptied himself" and became obedient to death (Philippians 2:7–8). It is the wonder of Israel's faith that (long before Jesus) the preoccupation of the *creator God* with *creaturely wellbeing* was taken to be definitional.

And then the text moves from affirmation to imperative: "You shall also love the stranger." The narrative basis for the command is that "You were strangers is the land of Egypt." But the ground for the imperative is that Israel shall be "like God," like the God who loves strangers! Israel is to do what God does and what God has done for Israel. We notice that in verse 16, moreover, the text appeals to the practice of circumcision, a defining mark of difference (!), as a ground for obedience that replicates God's way in the world. What a mouthful!

Thus we can see that in the very book of Deuteronomy that contains the purity code (14:3–21) and the catalogue of exclusions (23:1–8), we have a mandate to "welcome the strangers" that is an imitation of God who welcomes strangers. Thus *within* the book of Deuteronomy itself a principal tension for covenantal faith is articulated, a tension between *welcome* and *schismogenesis,* a *welcome* of the other and an *exclusion* of the other as a mark of identity. This tension is so poignantly voiced by Martha Nussbaum, in her book, *The Clash Within: Democracy, Religious Violence, and India's Future* (2007). She takes up the work of Samuel Huntington who has anticipated that we are headed for a deep conflict between "The West" and Islam. In his book, *The Coming Clash of Civilizations and the Remaking of World Order* (2011), Huntington assumes that the clash will be vigorous, violent, and dangerous. Contra Huntington, Nussbaum has studied the matter with reference to the conflict of Hindus and Muslims in India. She concludes that the most elemental "clash" that Huntington describes is not "out there" between tribes or nations or religious groups. It is rather a "clash within," thus the title of her book:

> We need not reject his [Gandhi's] insight that a "conflict of civilizations" is in the last instance always internal, an attempt to deal with the shame and fear of being human. . . . The real "clash of civilizations" is not "out there," between admirable Westerners and Muslim zealots. It is here, within each person, as we oscillate uneasily between self-protective aggression and the ability to live in the world with others. (333, 337)

Thus the "clash within" is "within each person" as it is "within" the book of Deuteronomy.

This awareness is a profound insight into our psychological processes of self-securing protection. It is also an important tool for pastoral work, and an identification of the hard work the church must do, namely, to assist each of us in identifying and processing the tension "within" concerning *exclusionary self-protection* and *openness to the other*. The ground for "exclusion as self-protection" is some "law," some measure of "righteousness" that the "other" never reaches. The capacity for welcome is the inexplicable gift of grace, an acknowledgment that all of us and each of us are grounded in unmerited love, mercy, and care from the Holy One. And we are, as Nussbaum states, engaged every day in processing that tension that we may do in crude or quite sophisticated ways.

I was led to this exposition by an op-ed piece in the *New York Times* by Rabbi Charlie Cytron-Walker, "My Synagogue Was Attacked, but I Will Never Stop Welcoming the Stranger" (February 23, 2022), the rabbi for Congregation Beth Israel in Colleyville, Texas. The rabbi and his congregants experienced the assault of a gunman from whom he and his congregants eventually, after a long standoff, escaped unharmed. The rabbi has reflected on this searing experience. He understands the assault, standoff, and escape belonging, as a dramatic whole, to the trajectory of "welcoming the stranger."

> *The command to care for the stranger is mentioned at least 36 times in the Torah, the first five books of the Bible—more than any other mitzvah. It's mentioned so often because we need the reminder, because it isn't natural. It is hard. Just getting past the notion of fearing the stranger is a big enough hurdle.*

Cytron-Walker avers that "current reality" is an endless procession of vigils and "gathering after gathering of mourning" after intentional acts of hate and violence. But then he writes:

I believe with all my heart and soul that we can—and must—change that reality. That goes back to caring for the stranger—caring enough that we're willing to meet and talk with those who are different from ourselves. Caring enough to know that while our experiences may not be the same, and that we will probably disagree, we are human beings with something to teach and something to learn. That is not easy. And right now, it feels countercultural. Many parts of Judaism are countercultural—especially the instruction that we do what is right, not what is easy. When it comes to the care with which we are supposed to treat other people, those teachings cross religious and cultural boundaries.

Just now we are witnessing an impressive, generous welcoming of the stranger concerning the refugees from Ukraine. Such an outpouring of generous welcome is a measure of what is possible for us. But of course such an extraordinary act is evoked only by the extraordinary crisis in Ukraine. For the most part, such generous welcome is not operative among us, certainly not in loci where there is fear of those who are "unlike us." And even in Ukraine, there are many reports of Black students there being badly treated or excluded as they try to escape to the West. For the most part our welcome is grudging and miserly.

Wading into this common ambivalence is clearly the work of the church. That work runs across the span from honest conversation to policy advocacy to fresh theological reflection. The case has to be made, over and over, that the God of the Gospel is not tribal or national, and is not allied with any racial or gender "purity." It is the truth of this God, shared by Jews and Christians (and well beyond those communities), that the great creator God is immediately and intensely in solidarity with the "unlike," with those who are unlike us.

It is not a surprise that "the stranger" shows up as a player in the formation of wellbeing in the parable of Jesus:

Come, you who are blessed by the Father, inherit the kingdom prepared for you from the foundation of the world; for I was hungry and you gave me food, I was thirsty and you gave me something to drink, I was a stranger *and you* welcomed *me, I was naked and you gave me clothing, I was in prison and you visited me.* (Matthew 25:34–36)

The list of indispensables for a working, workable creation is offered: *food, drink, welcome, clothing, care, and visitation.* The "big six" of those requiring attentive generosity include *the hungry, the thirsty, the stranger, the naked, the sick,* and *the prisoner.* It is easy enough to see that Jesus gets this basic list from the book of Deuteronomy. And the book of Deuteronomy derives its inventory from the transformative acts of God who is "down and dirty" with *food, drink, welcome, clothing, care, and visitation.*

The work to be done by faithful human agents derives from the disclosure of God in the Torah and, subsequently, in the teaching of Jesus. This "revelation" belongs on the lips of pastors, on the tongues of congregations, in the budgets of the church, and in the policies of the state. "The stranger" is the litmus test of sustainable wellbeing. The fear of the "unlike" needs to be identified and named. We need practice in acknowledging and processing our fear in the community. We need models of risk running. We have texts of truth-telling that must be endlessly parsed among us. We cannot make our way into wellbeing by being "schizoid" about our neighbors. That kind of fearful engagement has never worked. It will not work now. That is why we are summoned to "a more excellent way."

❧ 13 ❧

THE STRANGENESS
OF THE STRANGER

*When an alien resides with you in your land, you shall not
oppress the alien. The alien who resides with you shall be to you
as the citizen among you; you shall love the alien as yourself,
for you were aliens in the land of Egypt; I am the Lord your
God.* (Leviticus 19:33–34)

*You shall have one law (*mispat*) for the alien and for the citizen; for
I am the Lord your God.* (Leviticus 24:22)

*For the Lord your God is God of gods and Lord of lords, the great God,
mighty and awesome, who is not partial and takes no bribe, who exe-
cutes justice for the orphan and the widow, and who loves the strangers,
providing them food and clothing. You shall also love the stranger, for
you were strangers in the land of Egypt.* (Deuteronomy 10:17–19)

WHAT FOLLOWS IS a report on two books I have recently read, quite by
happenstance, back-to-back. The first book is *Of Fear and Strangers:
A History of Xenophobia* by George Makari (2021). This ambitious
book traces the notion of xenophobia (fear of the stranger) through
the history of Western Christianity. Makari arrives at most interesting
and important conclusions about his subject.

Because the term "xenophobia" smacks of old Greek etymology,
one might expect that xenophobia is a quite ancient enterprise. To
the contrary, Makari finds no compelling evidence for such an
ancient concern. Rather, in both Greek and Hebrew traditions one
finds an openness to strangers that runs toward "philioxenia," love

of the stranger. Makari observes that, in the tradition of Matthew, Jesus enjoins welcome to the stranger (*xenos*) (Matthew 25:35). Most important is the admonition of Hebrews 13:

> *Let mutual love* (philadelphia; *"love of brother") continue.*
> *Do not neglect to show hospitality to strangers* (philoxenias),
> *for by doing that some have entertained angels without*
> *knowing it.* (vv. 1–2)

Of most interest is the fact that "mutual love" (*philadelphia*) and "hospitality to strangers" (*philoxenias*) occur together, exactly an antithesis to *xenophobia*!

Without strong evidence in the ancient world, Makari judges that xenophobia is a more modern phenomenon. Specifically, he pegs its emergence in the coming modern world to the action and ambition of Isabella and Ferdinand in their effort to create a "pure Christian Spain" in the late fifteenth century. They did so by expelling Jews and Muslims who, perforce, fled, were converted to Christian faith, or were killed.

> *Catholicism became the rallying cry of the kingdom . . . . The*
> *nation's subjects would now be those with pure blood, with*
> *clear Christian ancestry . . . . Subjects were to be zealots in*
> *the pursuit of these national goals. Shared hatred of aliens*
> *and enemies pulled a diverse people together.* (19–21)

This drastic, ruthless royal initiative, moreover, is dated to exactly the same period as three other remarkable turns of public affairs:

- The *discovery of the New World* by Christopher Columbus, a subject of Isabella and Ferdinand who brought back to them much gold;
- The flourishing of the Church's *Inquisition* that sought out and punished all of those who were short of "pure faith"; and

- The papal "Doctrine of Discovery" that gave Spain privilege in the New World and provided that the "natives" must either convert or be killed.

It was readily concluded that non-Christians constituted a threat to the wellbeing of the pure Christian nation. The effective seizure of the New World by Spain signaled "the hegemony of their illusions" (22) (a wondrous phrase!) and legitimated their eager predatory quest for labor, markets, and gold that shaped the subsequent history of the New World. The legitimated ideology of this enterprise "unleashed mass murder of a different order" (22).

From this beginning Makari traces the practice of xenophobia through the emergence of nationalism in the eighteenth to nineteenth centuries:

> *Once feudal European states secularized and adopted more*
> *republican values, by which sovereignty was vested in the*
> *people. Weakened traditional elites and religious authorities,*
> *once wielding the crown and cross, could no longer as*
> *effectively use such time-honored methods to ensure social*
> *order. Into this vacuum, nationalism emerged with different*
> *self-defining strategies intended to cement the commitment of*
> *the citizenry.* (41)

From then on, the illusion of a homogeneous "pure" citizenry justified all kinds of exclusionary hostility toward "the other," that is, toward immigrants who could be perceived as a threat.

Makari exposits one other remarkable awareness. The European powers, in the wake of Columbus and his ilk, undertook aggressive colonizing of the non-European world, including the Americas, Asia, and Africa. They did so in the conviction of God-authorized righteousness:

> *Missionaries, school teachers, and functionaries carried the*
> *flags of freedom forward. They rubbed up against fortune*

> *hunters, ex-criminals, libertines, slave traders, and pirates.*
> *So confident were they in their righteousness, the good of*
> *their God, the supremacy of their lineage, and the superiority*
> *of their culture that the reaction of their hosts begat some*
> *confusion. Western travelers noted that in foreign lands, they*
> *would be met by accommodation and servile assistance, then*
> *suddenly rage and violence.* (53)

Eventually here and there, notably in China with the so-called Boxer Rebellion, some of the would-be colonized lands mounted resistance to Western "civilizing" pressure. Quite cleverly, Western propaganda, in the service of European predation, managed to label that resistance as "xenophobic," that is, resistance by China was parsed as "hostility to foreigners." This clever trick turned the tables on historical reality, for it was the West that refused foreigners. In defense of their own land and economy, the resistance of European colonization was labeled as "xenophobia."

More recent expressions of this tricky reversal have come in the form of claims that establish the inferiority of nonwhites, stereotypes that categorize second-class citizens, the notorious "church schools" that sought in violent ways to deculture native children, and finally genocide that exercised and justified wholesale elimination of the "other." Makari summarizes:

> *A decade after its invention, xenophobia had become a*
> *powerful biopolitical tool tied to science and race; it defined*
> *who was a primitive Easterner or Oriental, and who was*
> *a civilized Occidental Westerner. As applied by Western*
> *journalists, diplomats, experts, and observers, xenophobia*
> *was linked to a kind of primitivism that afflicted only the*
> *colonized, non-Europeans.* (67)

Most recently in our own context, this flag-waving *superiority-cum-violence* has been intolerantly preoccupied with non-European immigrants, culminating in the notorious Johnson–Reed Act of 1924 with its harsh exclusionary provisions. This sense of a white-European America being threatened by "others" has come to various expressions of nativism, not least the recent ideological chant, "We shall not be replaced." Indeed this fear-filled exclusionary ideology was given an even more notorious articulation when ex-President Trump spoke of the "quartette" of congressional women (Alexandria Ocasio-Cortez, Ilhan Omar, Rashida Tlaib, and Ayanna Pressley). In a statement that grossly diminished the presidency, Trump said:

> *Why can't they go back and help fix the totally broken*
> *and crime infested places from which they came?* (July 14,
> 2019)

He dared to say—so habituated in nativism is he—that he could not imagine that the four duly elected congresswomen are "from here." One can only conclude that xenophobia is alive and well, and at the brink of defining the United States under the banner, "Make America White Again."

There has of course been a steady stream of protests against this dangerous chauvinism. Makari in particular mentions Leo Tolstoy, Mark Twain, and Joseph Conrad.

But now the second book I note is *The Subversive Simone Weil: A Life in Five Ideas* by Robert Zaretsky (2021). Zaretsky presents the ideas of Weil, who was a radical public figure in France with dangerous words, dangerous ideas, and dangerous actions (1909–43). She wrote, spoke, and lived in solidarity with the exploited labor class in France. Among her "outrageous" ideas is this:

> *The essential nutrient for the flourishing of patriotism, as*
> *Weil sees it, is not pride, but compassion. Patriotism is fueled*
> *by sympathy, and not antipathy, for others.* (116)

Zaretsky can judge that her words are "bizarre," and slots his own comment alongside that of Charles de Gaulle who dismissed her words as those of a raving lunatic. Weil, of course, was not deterred by such dismissals, but kept to her conviction that was grounded in her Jewishness and in her embrace of Christian faith. She asserts that,

> *Compassion is an equal-opportunity sentiment, one that*
> *is able, without hindrance, to cross frontiers, extend itself*
> *over all countries in misfortune, over all countries without*
> *exception; for all peoples are subject to the wretchedness of our*
> *human condition. . . . We must not portray our country* [she
> means France] *that is not only beautiful and precious, but*
> *also is imperfect and very frail.* (117)

In this judgment of "patriotism as compassion" Weil is of course moving upstream against very heavy currents of opinion. To be sure, that does not deter her as she intends to upend the ideological claims of supremacy and privilege by focusing on the inescapable reality of the commonality of the human community. To uphold Weil's "compassion" as subversive of and alternative to conventional nationalism and ordinary imperialism is a very long shot. But of course it is a long shot on which human lives have always depended.

So, consider the subject of Makari and Zaretsky, of *xenophobia* and *compassion.* I have no doubt that we are compelled by gospel faith to weigh in on this interface. The simple claim, "Love thy neighbor," is at the heart of our ethical reflection. It is easy enough but no less urgent, I believe, to insist on this claim in the church. It is easy enough because it is a widely shared conviction across the spectrum of the church. No one will argue against that mandate. It is nevertheless urgent because the church, its members, and its pastors must be uncompromising about our most serious faith commitment at the center of which is the "other" whom God loves.

That, however, is not the hard work. The hard work, as every pastor knows, is to make the case that *the ethical primacy of the "other"* pertains not only to the privacy of faith but also to the body politic. We are now in a dangerous moment concerning the future shape of our society. The fears of exclusionary nativism are strong and encouraged by ample hidden money. The claim for the primacy of the stranger, however, is more elemental than anything that hidden money can propagate; the claim is grounded in nothing less than our shared, created, bodily commonality that refuses the false claims of eugenics, that resists the dismissive practices of stereotype, and that abhors the easy legitimacy of genocide.

Just now we as a society are engaged in a question about our future, about whether compassion, as a shared practice might impinge upon public policy and public practice. The force of nativism is of course all for compassion as long as it remains privatized so that we keep control of the process. But with compassion kept privatized, fear will always prevail in public matters over any substantive compassion. When compassion becomes a mark of public work, it issues in deeply felt justice initiatives and in greatly altered economic distribution. We must not forget that xenophobia is a not a virtue; it is a fear. It is a fear that our humanity is too frail for generosity and too vulnerable for social justice. We know better than that! That is why we pray for God's rule to come quickly "on earth as it is in heaven," a rule of consummate generosity and determined restorative justice. Beyond such a wondrous prayer, there are specific risks to run, policies to enact, and strangers to welcome. Faith does not linger in fear because it is confident that our future may indeed embrace a more excellent way. The phrase that lingers in my awareness is in the words of our almost-national anthem, "O Beautiful for Spacious Skies." It includes these amazing lines:

> *O beautiful for heroes proved in liberating strife,*
> *Who more than self their country loved, and mercy more than*
>   *life.* (*Glory to God* [2013], 338)

Imagine: "mercy more than life!" We sing, moreover, that even our "success" shall be "nobleness." Who knew?

🌿 14 🌿

UNEMANCIPATED!

RABBI SHARON BROUS, in "Imagine a Bible with No Moses, No Story of the Exodus" (*New York Times*, April 15, 2022), writes of the *Slave Bible* published in 1807. It was prepared by white masters for use among Black slaves. (A copy of it is located at Fisk University.) Brous reports that the white editors carefully determined what was appropriate reading for Black slaves in their worship. Of course the Bible had to be carefully edited for such usage because the Bible contains too much dangerous dynamite that would evoke Black energy, passion, and resolve. To that end, this racially inspired edition omitted mention of Moses and the Exodus. Thus the exclamation of Rabbi Brous: "Imagine!" It took white editors to imagine and implement such a deletion in and distortion of the Bible!

It is not difficult to see and understand what the white editors intended by this work. They wanted the Black slaves to have a vision of Christian faith that lacked the primal narrative of emancipation. They did not want available to the slaves a tale of freedom in which the people of God, organized and led by Moses, departed the unbearable slave camps and the harsh brick quotas of Pharaoh. They did not want on offer a model narrative in which one could agree to depart from and dismantle a predatory system that produced great wealth for the master via cheap (very cheap!) labor from those without power. They did not want psalms of emancipation and songs of freedom on the lips or in the ears of the slaves.

Most of all, they did not want the Lord of the Exodus alive and well in the worship and imagination of the slaves. They wanted instead that the Bible should bear witness to a God who established and legitimated an unchanging status quo in which every person was assigned a proper, abiding role. Without any acute or articulated hermeneutic, these editors understood that religious agitation of an emancipatory kind constituted an immediate and abiding threat to the status quo. Thus the Bible was, perforce, skewed in this rendering in order to preserve and authorize dominant economic interest. Once again, the values of the dominant class easily became the dominant values!

It is easy enough to be offended by and indignant at such a skewing of the biblical testimony, and such distortion of the character of God is given in the biblical narrative as the resolved uncompromising emancipator. Indeed the entire prophetic tradition of ancient Israel depends on this freedom of God, this divine refusal to be hemmed in by temple, liturgy, piety, doctrine, or ethic. It is this same God who can will, subsequently, the destruction of the holy city of Jerusalem, for this God has no defining attachment to any human socioeconomic political arrangement. Indeed, the freedom of God from the Roman Empire was the ground from which Jesus was raised from the dead, for the God of the Gospel refused to be contained in the lethal calculus of the empire. What is at stake in this work of these white editors is the freedom of God, that is, God's refusal to be contained in our best habits and formulations. It is inescapable that this deceitful editing of the Bible should promptly evoke our indignation concerning God's transformative freedom.

That much seems obvious. But then I took a deep breath and took a second look. Then it occurred to me that the deletion of the Exodus narrative from the working canon of Scripture is not simply an achievement of this white protection of a system of slavery. The same deletion, likely for the same reasons, is alive and well among us. (I could not remember the last time I had heard, in my characteristically white church setting, a sermon on the emancipatory Lord of the exodus.)

I decided to check out the usage of Scripture in my own denomination (UCC) that follows the Revised Common Lectionary. I simply looked to see what texts are designated for regular reading. I discovered that for the calendar year 2022, there is exactly one reading from the book of Exodus in the calendar, Exodus 35:29–35 on February 27. That is the only citation of the book of Exodus, and that reading is for "Transfiguration Sunday," so that the text serves to reinforce the luminous exposé of the transfigured Jesus in Luke 9:28–36. That single reading offers no reference to the tale of emancipation, even though in the Priestly texts of the book of Exodus pain is taken to link the *laborious Priestly regulations* to the *story of emancipation.* Concerning the God who authorizes punctilious worship regulations, the Priestly tradition declares:

> *And they shall know that I am the Lord their God, who brought them out from the land of Egypt, that I might dwell among them. I am the Lord their God.* (Exodus 29:46)

Even the Priestly writers bear witness to the emancipator, knowing that the freedom story can never be deleted from the tradition! Except that the lectionary committee has done just such a deletion!

To be sure, the UCC (Common) lectionary does better in 2020 where it offers a series of ten texts from the book of Exodus as a sequential reading in August to October. Even here, however, the dramatic exchange between Moses and Pharaoh concerning the plagues is missing, as are the triumphant songs of Moses and Miriam in chapter 15. The references cited are fragmentary and piecemeal. Most remarkably, the reading for October 4, 2020, is from Exodus 20 on the Ten Commandments, but only verses 1–4, 7–9, and 12–20. Thus the commandments concerning idols and the Sabbath are abbreviated, suggesting that Moses is too long-winded for the progressive church that can deal in summaries.

As I felt indignation toward those old white editors of the *Slave Bible,* I had to take stock of my own church. And when I did, I concluded that my own church, as an echo of those white editors, was doing the same deletion of the text, albeit in a gentler, softer way. I could think of three dimensions to this promiscuous work of deletion.

First, the lectionary committee that selects our texts has no real understanding of or interest in the Old Testament, and surely would not appreciate the founding narrative of emancipation. For the most part, Old Testament texts are selected only because they "pair" nicely with a New Testament reading, but have no intrinsic interest of their own. Thus it is no surprise that the narrative of emancipation never gets a full hearing.

Second and more important, I have no doubt that such selections of particular texts (and "deletion" of other texts) not only serve ancient white editors but also serve contemporarily to accommodate the biblical text to our preferred status quo. Of course we would not be as blatant as were they, but "liberals," I sense, much prefer a biblical text that is amenable to a capitalist system, and that is surely in sync with Enlightenment rationality. Thus the notion of an emancipatory God who is an active agent of revolutionary imagination is much too primitive for our tastes. Our epistemological preference, moreover, is no doubt a function of our economic, political commitment. We cannot imagine and do not want to imagine a God who is on the loose with sufficient power and authority to overthrow the Pharaonic system. Nor are we, for the most part, able to imagine that our economic system of individualized predation is simply a contemporary articulation of Pharaoh who is able and eager to create a totalizing system in which nothing is permissible outside our system, in other words, outside our control. Some go so far as to think, moreover, that even NATO is a stratagem to assure our US "mastery" of the political economy of the West in order to fend off disruption. The result is that much of our theology and its practice are privatized and domesticated to personal, familial matters, while our public stance in the church is largely an echo of dominant values. We do not intend it so. We never actually decided that. Rather, it is the relentless pressure of assumption that is commonly shared among us that delineates what of the Bible we can tolerate in our public worship and discourse.

Third, after the reductionist procedures of the lectionary committee, and after the slow relentless pressure of "common opinion," we may come to the actual work of the Bible in the life and practice of the congregation. Very many people come to church anticipating a presentation that will "fit in" with how they arrived at church. Pastors, moreover, are often either a part of "fitting in" ourselves, or we know better but dare not run many or great risks for the sake of dollars, members, and wellbeing.

The outcome of this triad of *lectionary indifference, the slow steady pressure of common opinion*, and *the actual reality of the congregational life*, in many instances, leads to a careful editing of the Bible so that the God of the Bible does not unduly rock the boat. One can observe this erosive domestication of God in the Bible itself, as when Solomon "captures" God in the temple where God will dwell "forever":

> *The Lord has said he would dwell in thick darkness.*
> *I have built you an exalted house,*
> *a place for you to dwell in forever.* (I Kings 8:12–13)

Or in the readiness of Amaziah, the priest, who can declare that his sanctuary is a "protected zone" where the freedom of God will not be allowed in a way that offends the king:

> *O seer, go, flee away to the land of Judah, earn your bread*
> *there, and prophesy there; but never again prophesy at*
> *Bethel, for it is the king's sanctuary, and it is a temple of the*
> *kingdom.* (Amos 7:12–13)

One can imagine those long-ago white masters being "safe and secure" from any "God danger" coming from among their slaves. *Mutatis mutandis*, one can imagine many church people in our society being "firm in the gospel" in a way that has no critical connection to the economic political realities of the day. So much for editing the Bible!

It is not for me to say what must be done in the midst of this default practice in the church. But two matters occur to me. First, the Christian congregation must be invited (subjected!) to the *reading of extended biblical texts* in which the full claim of the narrative is sounded concerning the God who inhabits the narrative. Alongside the full narrative, the church must do much singing of the songs of the great Exodus Psalms (Psalms 78:11–16, 105:26–42, 106:8–12, 136:10–15) so that our lips and our ears become familiar with the cadences of emancipated, energizing imagination concerning the God who will resist and refuse Pharaoh. As we do that, we will notice that the "incidental" rescues of Jesus (as in Luke 7:22) are all together a part of the Exodus deliverance he performed. As we do that, the congregation need not be so shocked when the gospel is shown to be implicated in many of the liberation movements all around us that assault the hegemony of our preferred white male control. But second, many congregations and many pastors have yet to do the hard work of learning and practicing a *critical hermeneutic* that connects old texts to contemporary socioeconomic realities in a sustained, credible, and summoning way. Our excessive preoccupation with "historical questions" has distracted us from the more demanding, more generative work of sociopolitical interpretation.

In the end, the God of the gospel will not be domesticated by our best learning or our most careful editing. Even Moses wanted to know God's name (Exodus 3:13)! If he could know God's name, he could "administer" God in ways that suited him and his interests. But God of course refused. God refused to disclose God's own name. Later on, God will refuse to show God's face to Moses (Exodus 33:20). God refuses to be "available" for the mastery of Moses because God will not let go of God's own freedom that allows God to emancipate from even the most toxic systems. In response to Moses's request for God's name, God utters an enigmatic formula that serves to keep the interpretive rabbis busy to this very day (Exodus 3:14). God will not be named or domesticated or contained in our preferred arrangements. This God goes "to and fro in the land" (II Samuel 7:6–7). How then shall we speak of this God? Well, how about this? "I am YHWH [NB: no vowels, thus unpronounceable], who brought you out of the land of Egypt, out of the house of bondage." That is the name! The name is a tag word for emancipation, and the Bible uncompromisingly embeds the *name* in the *narrative*. There are, to be sure, many other gods on offer. And we know their names and can call them out. Those gods, however, are weak, anemic, and impotent:

> *They have mouths, but do not speak;*
> *eyes, but do not see.*
> *They have ears, but do not hear;*
> *noses, but do not smell.*
> *They have hands, but do not feel;*
> *feet, but do not walk;*
> *they make no sound in their throats.* (Psalm 115:5–7)

And then the psalmist adds a most alarming verse:

> *Those who make them* [the idols] *are like them;*
> *so are all who trust in them.* (Psalm 115:8)

The worship of gods who are weak, anemic, and impotent produces worshippers who are in turn weak, anemic, and impotent, who lose agency and become spectators, and not participants in the historical process of emancipation. Such worship produces unengaged couch potatoes. What we get, if we yield to *the indifference of the lectionary committee, the slow pressure of common opinion,* and *the cocooning temptation of life in a congregation,* are idols that rob us of agency. We often prefer those other gods to the narrative of the rescuing God of emancipation. Pharaoh preferred other gods whose names he knew. None of that, however, could protect Pharaoh—or us—from the intrusive work of the God who continues to be emancipatory . . . on our behalf or in spite of us. For good reason Rabbi Brous urges us to "imagine" with an imagination that is not domesticated and not conforming to dominant interests. It turns out that the Bible is not designed for "masters." It is rather designed for slaves on their way to freedom where they may dance and sing and live in newly given wellbeing.

Part III

CIVIC MEMBERSHIP, RESPONSIBILITY, AND FAILURE

⚜ 15 ⚜

BONDS OF AFFECTION!

I am lothe [sic] *to close. We are not enemies, but friends. We must not be enemies. Though passion may have strained, it must not break our bonds of affection. The mystic chords of memory, streching* [sic] *from every battle-field, and patriot grave, to every living heart and hearthstone, all over this broad land, will yet swell the chorus of the Union, when again touched, as surely they will be, by the better angels of our nature.* (Abraham Lincoln, First Inaugural Address, March 4, 1861)

IMAGINE THESE WORDS at the brink of war! Lincoln still hoped to avert war. He still believed that the national bonds of unity might be more compelling than the deep divisions so obvious to all. He still hoped. And in his hope he called his fellow citizens to their better selves . . . their better angels. We may ponder those phrases! "Bonds of affection," the deep assumption of belonging with and belonging to and belonging for each other! "Mystical chords of memory" that appealed to a bold and courageous past in which there was daring solidarity with intent not only on "a more perfect union," but freedom from unfair taxation and freedom for westward expansion for "free soil," a cause so dear to Lincoln. There had been sufficient solidarity to continue to speak of shared dreams, shared risks, and shared duties. All of that was now at risk, and Lincoln refused to give in. Until the moment of the firing on Fort Sumpter, Lincoln continued to hope that a shared inheritance was stronger than what would drive the nation into a bloody violent war. In the end, the combination of self-assured ideology and economic ambition prevailed over Lincoln's poetically rendered national unity.

Great presidents count on such rhetoric to mobilize our better angels, rhetoric sometimes effective, sometimes disregarded via our smaller ideological agenda.

The phrase "bonds of affection" has drawn my sustained attention as I watched the hearing for Judge Ketanji Brown Jackson. I could think of three places in Scripture where we see the "bonds of affection" operating, though you might think of others as well. The first case of "bonds of affection" in Scripture that I cite is the friendship of Jonathan and David. Jonathan is the son of Saul, and therefore heir to that quite unstable throne. But his bond of affection for David overrode his loyalty to his father. At the outset we are told:

> *When David had finished speaking to Saul, the soul of Jonathan as bound to the soul of David, and Jonathan loved him as his own soul. . . . Then Jonathan made a covenant with David, because he loved him as his own soul.* (I Samuel 18:1,3)

Jonathan became an advocate for David in the face of Saul's great anger toward David:

> *Jonathan spoke well of David to his father Saul, saying to him, "The king should not sin against his servant David, because he has not sinned against you, and because his deeds have been of good service to you; for he took his life in his hand when he attacked the Philistines, and the Lord brought about a great victory for all Israel."* (19:4–5)

Jonathan took steps to assure David's loyalty to him and to his family:

> *If I am still alive, show me the faithful love of the Lord; but if I die, never cut off your faithful love from my house, even if the Lord were to cut off every one of the enemies of David*

> *from the face of the earth. Thus Jonathan made a covenant*
> *with the house of David, saying, "May the Lord seek out the*
> *enemies of David." Jonathan made David swear again by*
> *his love for him; for he loved him as he loved his own life.*
> (20:14–17)

In the face of that loyalty toward David, Jonathan nonetheless is fully engaged with his father and his two brothers in the battle against the Philistines. Indeed, he fights to the death in the cause of Israel and in the cause of his father, the king:

> *The Philistines overtook Saul and his sons; and the Philistines*
> *killed Jonathan and Abinadab and Malchishua, the sons of*
> *Saul.* (31:2)

Jonathan did not permit his bond of affection for David to distract from his commitment to Israel and to his father Saul.

The measure of their bonds of affection is deeply voiced in the lament on the lips of David who grieves over the deaths of Saul and Jonathan. For all his alienation from Saul, David can grieve at the same time for his friend, Jonathan, and for his king, Saul:

> *For there the shield of the mighty was defiled,*
> *the shield of Saul, anointed with oil no more.*
> *From the blood of the slain,*
> *from the fat of the mighty,*
> *the bow of Jonathan did not turn back,*
> *nor the sword or Saul return empty.*
> *Saul and Jonathan, beloved and lovely!*
> *In life and in death they were not divided;*
> *they were swifter than eagles,*
> *they were stronger than lions . . . .*
> *I am distressed for you, my brother Jonathan;*

greatly beloved to me;
your love was to me as wonderful,
passing the love of a woman. (II Samuel 1:21–26)

These deeply moving lines in their eloquence may indeed come from the lips of David. (We may leave aside for now the question of whether David and Jonathan had a gay relationship, as the evidence we have is inconclusive.) It is enough for us to see that the bonds of affection lasted through many toils and snares, and were not interrupted by the death of Jonathan.

The second scriptural case of the bonds of affection that I cite is in the narrative of Ruth. Naomi, an Ephrathite, had two sons who lived with her in Moab. Not surprisingly, the two sons married Moabite women. The family was disrupted when Elimelech, the husband of Naomi and the father of Mahlon and Chilion, died. After that the two sons died as well, leaving Naomi and her two daughters-in-law all as widows. Naomi resolved to return back to the land of Judah. She urged her two Moabite daughters-in-law to remain in Moab among their own people, as Naomi could not provide for them and they would have no future with her. One daughter-in-law, Orpah, complied with Naomi's mandate and chose to remain with her own family in Moab. The story turns, however, on the desire of the other Moabite daughter-in-law, Ruth, to remain with Naomi and return with her to be with her in Judah, in Bethlehem.

In her refusal to accept the counsel of Naomi, Ruth utters one of the most remarkable articulations of thick affection that bound her to Naomi:

Do not press me to leave you
or to turn back from following you!
Where you go, I will go;
Where you lodge, I will lodge;
your people shall be my people,

and your God my God.
Where you die, I will die—
There I will be buried.
May the Lord do thus and so to me,
and more as well,
if even death parts me from you! (Ruth 1:16–17)

We are given no commentary on this decisive utterance. Nor has anything in the narrative prepared us for this response. Perhaps she even surprised Naomi. The four terse lines concern *travel* ("go"), *residence* ("lodge"), *community solidarity* ("people"), and *faith* ("God"). The detail is complete and covers every possible aspect of their relationship:

Where you go, I will go;
Where you lodge, I will lodge;
your people shall be my people,
and your God my God.

Ruth is committed to that companionship, and upon her resolve the rest of the story depends. Naomi apparently could see that Ruth was exceptionally resolved and made no further attempt to dissuade her from her decision:

When Naomi saw that she was determined to go with her, she said no more to her. (v. 18)

What follows is settlement in Bethlehem (1:19), marriage to Boaz (4:13), and the birth of a son, Obed (4:17). It is beyond the dramatic reach of the narrative to notice that from Obed, son of a Moabite, came David, son of Jesse, king of Israel (4:18–20). This outcome is of course reiterated in the genealogy of Matthew 1:5 (see I Chronicles 2:12).

It was the bonds of affection that drew Ruth to Naomi, to Judah, to Bethlehem, and finally to an indispensable contribution to the anticipated royal line. Naomi was wise enough not to disrupt these bonds, and Boaz had no reticence in accepting these bonds of affection that, within the narrative, readily override any problem with Ruth's foreign rootage. These bonds override what we might take to be a "natural" impediment to Ruth's resolve. These impediments are overruled by Naomi and Boaz.

The third example in Scripture of the bonds of affection that I cite concerns Paul's intimate connection to his congregation at Philippi. It is often noted that of all of Paul's epistles, it is his letter to the Philippian church that most evidences affection. Most of his congregations were quarrelsome, offended him, or received stern reprimand from him. But not to the Philippians:

> *It is right for me to think this way about all of you, because you hold me in your heart, for all of you share in God's grace with me, both in my imprisonment and in the defense and confirmation of the gospel. . . . I rejoice in the Lord greatly that now at last you have revived your concern for me; indeed, you were concerned for me, but had no opportunity to show it. . . . You Philippians indeed know that in the early days of the gospel, when I left Macedonia, no church shared with me in the matter of giving and receiving, except you alone.* (1:17–8, 4:10, 15)

It is this congregation more than any other that has been in full and faithful solidarity with Paul. These are his best friends, and he can count on them. Thus Paul sprinkles throughout his letter the address, "beloved." But of course this solidarity Paul cherishes with the Philippians concerns much more than mere friendship. What binds him to them and them to him is their shared commitment to and passion for the truth of the gospel. Thus Paul commends them to a life of glad obedience to the gospel that will enable the congregation to overcome every rift or dispute. Finally he writes to them:

Therefore, my brothers and sisters, whom I love and long for,
my joy and crown, stand firm in the Lord in this way, my
beloved. (4:1)

"Standing firm" is the grounding of their bonds of affection.

In these three instances—David and Jonathan, Naomi and Ruth, Paul and the Philippians—we can observe the force of the bonds of affection to override whatever impediment there may have been to solidarity and friendship. Thus Jonathan stood with David in spite of a more "natural" bond with his father, Saul. Thus Ruth readily and willingly forewent solidarity with her Moabite family for the sake of companionship with Naomi, the Israelite, a future with a people other than her own people. And Paul was able to find among the Philippians affection and solidarity that moved against the seemingly inescapable tendency of his congregations to compromise in serious ways the mandates of his gospel.

Thus Lincoln's mighty phrase, "bonds of affection," rings true in each of these relationships. "Bonds of affection," as Lincoln surely knew, could be powerful enough to contain the centrifugal force of hostility and alienation in his tense circumstance. He uttered the phrase on March 4, 1861, just a short bit before the firing on Fort Sumpter on April 12, 1861, that initiated the Civil War. Lincoln hoped against the facts on the ground. He believed that the "better angels" could override the force of alienation that was already well advanced. In this, Lincoln was deeply and immediately disappointed.

But his hope lingered. Nowhere did it linger more powerfully than in the eloquent romanticism of Walt Whitman. As late as 1900, long after the war, Whitman continued to champion the "bonds of affection" that Lincoln had celebrated. Whitman noticed that the nation, "as a state," could not be held together by lawyers, paper agreements, or arms. He knew that the only coherence that was sustainable for the state was to be found in friendship and affection:

> *Were you looking to be held together by the lawyers?*
> *By an agreement on a paper? Or by arms? . . .*
> *There shall come from me a new friendship—It shall be called*
>   *after my name,*
> *It shall circulate through The States, indifferent of place,*
> *It shall twist and intertwist them through and around each*
>   *other—*
> *Compact shall they be, showing new signs,*
> *Affection shall solve every one of the problems of freedom,*
> *Those who love each other shall be invincible.**

Whitman deliberately named states north and states south who had been at war, who will be a commonwealth of affection:

> *One from Massachusetts shall be comrade to a Missourian,*
> *One from Maine or Vermont, and a Carolinian and an*
>   *Oregonese,*
> *shall be friends triune, more precious to each other than all the*
>   *riches of the earth.*
> *To Michigan shall be wafted perfume from Florida,*
> *To the Mannahatta from Cuba or Mexico,*
> *Not the perfume of flowers, but sweeter, and wafted beyond*
>   *death.*

He deliberately named states north and south who will be comrades, "friends triune."

This of course is hard to imagine. It is hard to imagine affection now, between Massachusetts and Missouri, between Elizabeth Warren and Josh Hawley. It is difficult to think of any congeniality between Vermont and Carolina, between Bernie Sanders and Lindsay Graham.

---

* Walt Whitman, *Leaves of Grass*, published in various editions between 1855 and 1892. I came to this poem through an incidental reference by Parker Palmer.

But it is Whitman's hope. It is Lincoln's abiding hope. It is the promise of states united in affection. Such affection is a risk, as Jonathan risked beyond his father to David, as Ruth risked past her own family to Naomi, and as Paul risked toward his beloved Philippians. The "bonds of affection" depend upon identification of what is commonly held among us, and insistence that what is commonly held among us is more powerful than what readily divides us.

It is hard to imagine! But that is exactly what the gospel imagines. The gospel imagines that we are bodily creatures, all of us, held in the palm of the hand of the creator (the one who has the whole world in his hands). The more we focus on shared bodily reality (and away from distorting ideology), the more important are those bonds. It is the work of the gospel community to expose the phony force of ideology (Right or Left!) and to celebrate the common human requirements of compassion, mercy, and justice without which we cannot live. The more the church spends its energy on linguistic quibbles and quarrels over words and disputes about structures and organizational charts, the less power and moral energy it has for its proper missional engagement. Thus when we focus on our shared bodily reality and away from our favorite ideology, it is not so hard to imagine folk from Missouri and Massachusetts, from Vermont and Carolina being commonly concerned for bodily safety and well-being, for food, clothing, water, housing, and health. Friendship is the recognition that we all require these same props for wellbeing, every one of us! The matters that divide us are not primary. It may be the work of the church, in quite local settings, to invite conversation about our most elemental requirements, how they are to be delivered and allocated. When the "other" is addressed and taken seriously as "beloved," as Paul did his friends in Philippi, as Jonathan did toward David, and as Ruth did with Naomi—beloved by us, beloved by God, beloved by those who we have taken as enemy, we may be led to a stunning generosity. Our capacity for affection must not be driven underground by our ideological zeal. When we can maximize our affection toward the beloved of God, we are our "better selves," led by our "better angels." That must be what Lincoln had in mind!

And even as he drew near the end of his presidency, the end of the war, and the end of his life, Lincoln was a hoper:

> *With malice toward none; with charity for all; with firmness in the right, as God gives us to see the right, let us strive on to finish the work we are in; to bind up the nation's wounds; to care for him who shall have borne the battle, and for his widow and his orphan—to do all which may achieve and cherish a just, and a lasting peace, among ourselves and with all nations.* (Second Inaugural Address, March 4, 1865)

Just eleven days after, on March 15, 1865, Lincoln answered Thurlow Weed who had commended him for his speech. He wrote to Weed:

> *I expect the latter* [his second inaugural address] *to wear as well as—perhaps better than—any thing I have produced; but I believe it is not immediately popular. Men are not flattered by being shown that there has been a difference of purpose between the Almighty and them. To deny it, however, in this case, is to deny that there is a God governing the world.* ("To Thurlow Weed," in *Speeches and Writings 1859–1865* [n.d.], 689)

This is enough to ponder amid our political divisions: "There is a difference of purpose between the Almighty and them." We may bet on the purpose of the Almighty that is marked by affection, friendship, and neighborliness. Whatever contradicts that is open to severe questioning, whether in Missouri or Massachusetts, in Vermont or in Carolina.

"BONDS OF AFFECTION"...
ONCE MORE

I RECENTLY WROTE an exposition of the phrase from Lincoln's First Inaugural Address, "the bonds of affection." Lincoln hoped that those "bonds of affection" would override the eagerness for war. I considered how Lincoln's phrase was explicated in the poetry of Walt Whitman and concluded that the recovery of such "bonds" is now urgent among us. Since I wrote that piece, I have become aware of two books that in very different ways explore Lincoln's phrase amid our ongoing national history. My purpose here is to call attention to these two titles. I do so because it is evident that all such bonds that make our democratic society workable are now among us frayed almost beyond recognition.

The first of these two books has the title, *Bonds of Affection: Civic Charity and the Making of America—Winthrop, Jefferson, and Lincoln*, and was written by Matthew Holland (2007). Holland takes up in turn the words of these three leaders who shaped the formation and definition of the United States. He shows how among them there is both commonality and major differences:

> *At the height of their influence, all three figures delivered
> a seminal speech appealing to certain communal bonds
> of affection which they argued were essential to a stable,
> flourishing polity. In attempting to draw out and sustain these
> bonds of affection, each leader consciously worked to channel
> some understanding of Christian love—what the New
> Testament calls "charity" (I Cor. 13:13)—into a central civic,
> rather than strictly religious virtue. In doing so, they helped*

> *establish a unique and important strain in the American*
> *political tradition . . . . (5)*

This shared appeal to "charity" is rooted in the Greek New Testament word, *agape*, that concerns love of God and love of neighbor. As the term was variously used, however, its meaning was adapted, mostly in a departure from the meaning it had in the New Testament. Even as he appreciates the common use of the term "charity," Holland is candid in identifying sustained resistance to the conclusion that such "charity" could be generative in civic society:

> *Machiavelli's political realism, Bacon's scientific materialism,*
> *Locke's philosophical liberalism, Freud's therapeutic justice,*
> *and Nietzsche's radical skepticism of any traditionally*
> *understood moral norms all remain exceptionally strong*
> *influences in our post-Christian present. Together they*
> *form—whatever their differences—a most imposing barrier*
> *for charity to play any meaningful part in the formation of*
> *an important civic ideal. (12)*

After this acknowledgment, nonetheless, Holland goes on to consider how appeal to such "charity" might be an effective civic effort, as even George W. Bush could appeal to a "compassionate conservatism."

The first of these three leaders identified by Holland is John Winthrop, longtime governor of the Massachusetts Bay Colony. In 1630 Winthrop delivered a speech (sermon) as the *Arbella* moved into the harbor, a speech that Holland terms "America's first great speech" (27). In his address Winthrop unapologetically appealed to the New Testament notion of *agape* ("charity") that he took as the foundation of all civic virtues. He voiced a strong sense of divine providence that supported the founding of the colony, and insisted that "charity" is a required practice in response to the faithful generosity of divine providence. Holland opines that Winthrop, in his exposition, drew upon an earlier *Christian Dictionary* that asserted that charity is,

> *that* affection *of love which moves us to hold our neighbors*
> *dear, and to desire and seek their good in everything which is*
> *dear unto them, and that for Christ and his sake, according*
> *to the will of God.* (45)

What is most striking in Winthrop's articulation is the ready appeal to the governance of God in civic affairs, and the insistence that *agape* was the appropriate response to the generosity of God. Winthrop said and believed that the will of the providential God was at work among the colonialists and that this same God summoned the people to the work of "charity."

When we come to Holland's second case, Jefferson, matters have changed decisively. Jefferson will no longer appeal to Christian doctrine, and will allow for "divine providence" in only the most generic and formal way. His bent toward a "natural" deism precluded any serious appeal to the substance of Winthrop's address. Thus in the Declaration of Independence, Jefferson does not appeal to divine governance or guidance, but to the right time in the course of human events for human initiative. The combat to which the colonialists are summoned by Jefferson is not to the purpose of God but to the loyalty for and with each other. Jefferson does indeed urge the practice of "charity" for the sake of the democracy. But this "charity" is quite different from that of Winthrop and concerns community solidarity without reference to the deity.

Being informed by the previous work of James Madison, Jefferson eventually could insist that the democracy depended upon mutual affection:

> *As time marched on, Jefferson himself stepped up to say*
> *how necessary national bonds of affection are to sustain*

> *liberal American democracy. At one point, he even turned*
> *to Christianity in some form to try to refashion a national*
> *character apparently so lacking in mutual affection as to*
> *threaten his cherished aim of a model natural liberty.* (122)

It seems, however, that every time we may make such an interpretation of Jefferson, we must promptly retract or modify. Thus Holland judges:

> *But even here, it must be stressed that Jefferson never fully*
> *embraced any* traditional *version of charity. Virtually all*
> *traditional biblical interpretations of* caritas *emphasize that*
> *man's love of God and neighbor is only made possible, and*
> *becomes obligatory, by God's first loving man. . . . Since*
> *Jefferson never accepted the divinity of Christ or the doctrine*
> *of atonement, God's graceful and obliging love is explicitly*
> *absent from his ideal of* caritas. (135)

While Jefferson primarily appealed to classical tradition in the Declaration, Holland observes:

> *But surely there is also something of the* agapic *in this*
> *rhetoric. The Book of John records that on the night of his*
> *Last Supper, Jesus meets with his apostles and discourses on*
> *many things, including a vital emendation to his previous*
> *teachings on charity. That night he gives his disciples a "new*
> *commandment" revising the old commandment to love your*
> *neighbor as yourself. Now, he says, the principle is "love one*
> *another, as I have loved you" (John 13:34).* (119)

Thus we can see how Winthrop's legacy of divinely rooted *agape* lingers for Jefferson, as it would continue to linger for the democracy long after Jefferson. Jefferson nevertheless gives voice to a general uneasiness about connecting the dots too clearly from God's providence to the working of democracy. He is, by the end of his work, finally aware that the entire enterprise requires "affection," or democracy becomes impossible. In such a way Jefferson surely prepares the way for Lincoln's classic articulation.

In important ways Lincoln reiterates the ambivalence of Jefferson. On the one hand, he knows that mutual affection is the ground of a viable democracy. On the other hand, not unlike Jefferson, he is most reluctant to make any direct theological claims or connections, as his own stance is very close to an appreciative agnosticism. In his address to the Young Men's Lyceum in Springfield, Illinois (January 27, 1838), Lincoln put his accent on obedience to the law, all law, even bad law. In a statement that seems anticipatory of our insurrection on January 6, Lincoln could say in that address:

> *There is no grievance that is a fit object of redress by mob law. . . . Another reason which once was; but which, to the same extent, is now no more, has done much in maintaining our institutions thus far. I mean the powerful influence which the interesting scenes of the revolution had upon the passions of the people as distinguished from their judgment. . . . While the deep rooted principles of hate, and the powerful motive of revenge, instead of being turned against each other, were directed exclusively against the British nation. . . . But this state of feeling must fade, is fading, has faded, with the circumstances that produced it.* (33, 35)

At the end of his speech he declared:

> *Passion has helped us; but can do so no more. It will in the future be our enemy. Reason, cold, calculating, unimpassioned reason must furnish all the materials for our future support and defense. Let those materials be moulded*

into general intelligence, sound morality, *and, in particular,*
a reverence for the constitution and laws. (36)

As he matured in his presidential authority, Lincoln became
more willing to talk of the governance of God that had a more biblical
ring. In his First Inaugural Address he could speak of the urgency of
the "bonds of affection" as indispensable for democracy. Concerning
his Emancipation Proclamation, Holland observes:

> *The actual words of the Emancipation Proclamation*
> *may indeed be considered morally vapid, but the process*
> *that produced those words was governed by* agapic *ideals,*
> *running from heartfelt compassion for human slaves to a*
> *devout desire to follow the will of God. The document is, for*
> *Lincoln, a clear civic expression of his love for man and God*
> *articulated in the most careful way given the political and*
> *constitutional constraints he honored. It is an early political*
> *expression of Lincoln's new charity—one that sutures a*
> *soulful desire to act in concert with divine direction to an*
> *already acute care for his fellow human beings, all of whom*
> *(free and slave, North and South) he regarded as naturally*
> *entitled to liberty and all of whom, including himself,*
> *were obligated to follow the laws of the land—especially*
> *constitutional law.* (211–12)

In this judgment he had behind him the model of "Tom" in *Uncle
Tom's Cabin*, of whom Holland writes:

> *Tom's deep wellspring of pure love for God and others*
> *inspires in him a malice-free, suffering patience in the*
> *face of Southern injustice, yet by having their own*
> *Christian sentiments of human compassion broadened*
> *and deepened by Tom's example. . . . That the charity of*

> *Stowe's influential novel closely prefigures that of Lincoln's*
> *best speech and final moments suggests that a potent*
> *and complex sense of Christian love was vital in leading*
> *America into and then out of its bloodiest conflict, the*
> *national survival of which capped the creation of American*
> *democracy.* (167)

All of this development in Lincoln's thought culminates in his Second Inaugural Address that ends in a ringing summons of "charity for all" in order that there may come a lasting and just peace among the nations. Holland concludes of this address:

> *A profound reverence for God, an earnest desire to be in*
> *harmony with him—sacral expressions of* agape's *command*
> *to love God—abound in this address more than in any other*
> *presidential inaugural, maybe any other presidential speech*
> *of any kind. A willingness to forgive an enemy, an active and*
> *heartfelt sense of compassion for human suffering—moving*
> *expressions of* agape's *command to love neighbor as self—*
> *similarly stand out here above all other presidential rhetoric. . . .*
> *The* caritas *of Lincoln's Second Inaugural interdicts a spirit*
> *of hatred and revenge on both sides and elicits a miraculous*
> *response of forgiveness and benevolence, undoubtedly helping*
> *to rekindle the "bonds of affection" he pleaded for in his First*
> *Inaugural.* (234–35)

In the end, we have come nearly full circle to Winthrop's affirmation, though it is unmistakable that Lincoln's usage of such rhetoric is much less than a full embrace of Christian claims. He could indeed affirm "civic religion," but he would not fully accommodate exclusionary confessional claims. More recent experience has taught us that when faith claims become confessional in civic discourse, they inevitably become exclusionary and divisive. Given this reality as well as their own theological reticence, Jefferson and Lincoln refused full articulation of such claims, though it is equally clear that they made a more general appeal to precisely such claims.

From the soaring rhetoric of these three figures, the second book I mention, *Bonds of Affection: Americans Define Their Patriotism*, edited by John Bodnar (1996), takes us "down and dirty" into the realities of American politics. This book is a collection of essays by a variety of scholars who explore particular themes that constitute their research specialties. This collection is wide ranging, but nevertheless focuses on two general observations:

1. The notion of "bonds of affection" is a highly contested matter, with rivals seeking to occupy for themselves general civic claims.
2. Each particular advocate for "bonds of affection" sought not only the common good but, at the same time, also a particular advantage for their party or cause:

> *Our bonds of affection have always been subjected to complex interpretations. The earliest view of a virtuous nation of equals gave way by the late nineteenth century to a dream of a powerful nation rooted in the desires of powerful men and women who supported it for order and moral certainty at home and in the world. . . . In this version true patriots were often represented as male warriors. . . . Because all people and groups are susceptible to the attractions of power and justice, and because both coexisted in the language of patriotism, its appeal frequently crossed class, ethnic, regional, and gender borders and took unexpected turns. Citizens used patriotism for good and for malice. Thus this history of patriotism cannot be confused with our society's endless call for patriotism by voices that are more often partisan than they appear.* (11–12)

In order to exhibit the wide variations and aggressive appeals for "bonds of affection," below I will mention some of the topics explored in this generative collection.

The settlement of hostilities after the Civil War was a hope for Lincoln, "with malice toward none and charity for all." Cecilia Elizabeth O'Leary, in "'Blood Brotherhood': The Racialization of Patriotism, 1865–1919," explores the postwar struggle and sees that race was a defining factor in the settlement:

> *The GAR used a language of consensus, but beneath claims to a universal and inclusive Americanism, racial divisions deepened.* (69)

Appeal to "the Lost Cause" helped to shape the ideology of the New South and entrenched racism into the political memory of patriotism.

Andrew Neather, in "Labor Republicanism, Race, and Popular Patriotism in the Era of Empire, 1809–1914," considers the impact of labor (and labor unions) on the meaning of patriotism. Labor leaders sought to equate Americanism with support of unions, and for a time were successful in this equation. But Neather also recognizes the vexed nature of that patriotism:

> *Race created similar contradictions at the heart of labor republicans' formulations of citizenship and patriotism. Racial ideology was played out politically in the context of battles to exclude workers of color from unions and to ban Asian immigrants. All the railroad brotherhoods and most AFL unions routinely excluded African Americans, Latinos, and Asians.* (87)

Stuart McConnell, in "Reading the Flag: A Reconsideration of the Patriotic Clubs of the 1890s," reports on the struggle for patriotism at the end of the nineteenth century, especially given the rise of nativism. The upshot was an uneasy convergence of nativism, middle-class consciousness, and patriotism. McConnell describes the tension between an "ideology of sameness" and an "ideology of obligation" (105). The ideology of sameness that long prevailed was determinative of membership in state and in society:

> *National loyalty was mediated through ethnic and class hierarchies, with certain groups privileged to dictate the terms of entry to others. The ideology was one of ethnic and class similarity. Americanism was defined by such things as light skin, English-language ability, "Anglo-Saxon" ancestry, and social position in the established middle class.* (117–18)

The ideology of obligation asked what citizens owed to each other. But it is the "ideology of sameness" that was more persuasive, so much so that McConnell can conclude:

> *The patriotic clubs of the 1890s set in motion the process of narrowing national loyalty to the brackish channel in which it now runs. If we are seriously to rethink the meaning of national loyalty, then we must recover some of the complexity that was there before.* (119)

Kimberly Jensen, in "Women, Citizenship, and Civic Sacrifice: Engendering Patriotism in the First World War," explores the role of women in the sustenance of American democracy. The rising legitimacy of women as public players has been a long, slow process, often connected to women's participation in war. Their participation has served to accent the point of sacrifice; at the same time such a gradual expansion of the role of women has regularly been a significant challenge to the status quo:

> *The woman at arms threatened gender relations and women's roles in America at the same time that she symbolized their changing status.* (156)

Robert Westbrook, in "In the Mirror of the Enemy: Japanese Political Culture and the Peculiarities of American Patriotism in World War II," chronicles the shameless treatment of Japanese Americans during World War II. Even such a distinguished journal as *The Christian Century* joined in the silly caricature of the Japanese and their "emperor worship" (217). Westbrook opens his essay with these words:

> *There is nothing like a war to concentrate the minds of citizens on the meaning of patriotism, national identity, and political obligation.* (211)

Unfortunately, that "concentration" had sadly negative outcomes.

Wendy Kozol, in "'Good Americans': Nationalism and Domesticity in *Life* Magazine, 1945–1960," traces the cultural development, in the wake of World War II, of the notion of "good Americans," as those who fit readily into patriarchal social arrangements, supporting, in the home, the work of men in the economy. Richard Nixon as vice president notably characterized the new immigrants who arrived in the United States as "the kind of people who make good Americans" (241). Kozol observes:

> *The photo essay* [concerning the Csillag family in *Life* magazine] *encodes patriarchal values central to some of the most prevalent hegemonic narratives in American culture, ... Other photographs of the mother shopping and the father at work similarly visualize stereotypical gender roles.* (241)

George Lipsitz, in "Dilemmas of Beset Nationhood: Patriotism, the Family, and Economic Change in the 1970s and 1980s," considers Ronald Reagan and George W. Bush, who worked at "recovery" from the "Vietnam syndrome" that took the Vietnam War as a failure and a cause for national shame and embarrassment. The "New Patriotism" championed US military might that was put on modest exhibit in the skirmishes in Grenada and Panama. This accent led to the production of many "war movies," including *Rambo* with Sylvester Stallone. Lipsitz comments:

> *Stallone actually spent the Vietnam War as a security guard*
> *in a girl's school in Switzerland, but like Pat Buchanan,*
> *Newt Gingrich, Dick Chaney, David Stockman, and Rush*
> *Limbaugh—all of whom conveniently avoided military*
> *service themselves—Stallone established credentials as a*
> *"patriot" in the 1980s by retroactively embracing the Vietnam*
> *War and ridiculing those who had opposed it.* (256–57)

Neoconservatives helped to construct a "wanna be" world that had little connection to social reality. Reagan prospered through military posturing, even though he had, in Grenada, only defeated "the local police force and a Cuban army construction crew" (256).

Barbara Truesdell, in "Exalting "U.S.ness": Patriotic Rituals of the Daughters of the American Revolution," reports on the ideology and impact of the Daughters of the American Revolution, who claimed for themselves a peculiarly exalted notion of patriotism that has within it the seeds of denigration of many other citizens. Truesdell observes of the posturing of the DAR:

> *Within this symbolic cultural matrix, civil religion connects*
> *hegemonic ends and more intimate realms of experience*
> *through vernacular images and ideas . . . and provides the*
> *populace with the illusion that the right forces are in control.*
> *Alliance with hegemonic power bestows reflected power on the*
> *women who serve it and lends transcendent meanings to the*
> *members' everyday lives and to their vision of their roles in*
> *American society.* (275)

I have taken so long and given so much attention to detail in this collection because I believe it is a most useful commentary on our "bonds of affection." It is a shock to plunge from the noble, stately rhetoric of Winthrop, Jefferson, and Lincoln into the nitty-gritty of our civic realities. This collection shows how every dimension of the "bonds of affection" has been vigorously contested over time, with one interest group or another fiercely attempting to gain advantage over another.

In the midst of this hard-fought, ongoing contestation sits the church. The church is inescapably a party to this contestation, even as it lives beyond such contestation with its originary *"agape-*charity" textual tradition. The church is the only community that has as a part of its canon the command to "love one another" (John 13:34). And indeed, the church is the only community that has in its corpus the wondrous, too often reiterated, "love chapter" in I Corinthians 13. Imagine: this "love chapter" as a civic charter for the "bonds of affection":

> *Love is patient;*
> *love is kind;*
> *love is not envious or boastful or arrogant or rude.*
> *It does not insist on its own way;*
> *it is not irritable or resentful;*
> *it does not rejoice in wrong doing!*

It is most unfortunate that this lyrical utterance has been trivialized by its overuse at weddings, when in fact it might be a guide for the production and maintenance of civic bonds of affection. Methinks it might be a good idea to ban its use at weddings and preserve it for important civic occasions such as the Fourth of July and Thanksgiving. When used in that way, we may see that our "bonds of affection" require such generosity. This is surely what Winthrop, Jefferson, and Lincoln had in mind when they spoke of "charity" and commended bonds of affection that they insisted were deeper and more elemental than our civic disputes. This may be a time when the church can faithfully insist that its tradition of *agape*-charity is urgent in our civic practice. Without it, the rest is simply posturing and empty rhetoric. But of course Winthrop, Jefferson, and Lincoln all assumed and insisted that such matters were necessary practices and not empty rhetoric. Such bonds of affection are the most elemental stuff of democratic life. The church has a crucial role to play in the recovery of such charity. But the church can perform that role only when it gives up its attraction to individualized romantic sentimentalism.

❦ 17 ❦

HOMEGROWN TALIBAN!

THIS JUST IN ("Taliban Order Women to Cover Up Head to Toe," by Kathy Gannon, *Record Eagle*, May 8, 2022, 5A)! The Taliban just now are requiring all women in Afghanistan to wear head-to-toe clothing with only their eyes visible and to go out into public only when necessary. The prescribed punishment for violation of this harsh edict is to be wrought on male relatives, as though the women themselves are not worthy of such notice by the state. To our Western eyes such actions strike us as barbaric and grotesque, a rolling back in brutal ways of the few freedoms gained recently in Afghanistan.

Except—in the same week as the Taliban ruling in Afghanistan—we in the United States got the draft of Justice Alito's opinion to roll back in brutal ways recently gained rights in the United States with the overturning of *Roe v. Wade*. It could be that the Taliban action and Alito's draft opinion occurred in the same week only by coincidence. It could be, but we may doubt it. The two matters are a part of a vigorous, worldwide reassertion of patriarchy that occurs in many places under authoritarian regimes. I take it that Alito's opinion belongs to that worldwide enterprise. It flies under the compelling banner of "pro-life," but the moment should be recognized for what it is, not at all "pro-life," but anti-abortion and anti-woman. This is evident in the willingness of some in the movement to commit violence for the cause. It is more unmistakably evident in the lack of interest in or indifference of many who want to protect "the unborn child" but who have no interest at all in the "born child." At the moment that the movement celebrates the "unborn child," it steadfastly refuses any government investment in the wellbeing of the born child—not for adequate schools, not for secure health care, indeed, not for any of the measures that could contribute to the flourishing of our "born children."

The Taliban and Alito's opinion together agree that women's bodies should be controlled and administered by men through the power of the state. That claim of subordination (and consequent repression) has long received support for an overreading of Genesis 2 that counts women as subordinate, and a willful misreading of Ephesians 5 that concerns submissive subordination by women.

But we know better. Beginning with the intrepid work of Phyllis Trible (*God and the Rhetoric of Sexuality* [1979] and *Texts of Terror: Literary-Feminist Readings of Biblical Narratives* [1984]), followed by a host of compelling feminist and womanist interpreters, we are able to see quite clearly the trajectory of the emancipation and empowerment of women that runs through the Bible. Justice Alito has decreed that the only ones with assured constitutional rights are plantation owners and other property-owning white males. But our Holy Book asserts otherwise and denies any biblical affirmation to such subordination and repression of women.

It is not possible or necessary to focus on any single text in the Bible, though many surely occur to one. For now, if I were to focus on one text, it would be the exposition of the public woman in Proverbs 31:10–31. My well-beloved colleague, Christine Yoder, has written the classic study of this text, *Wisdom as a Woman of Substance: A Socio-economic Reading of Proverbs 1–9 and 31:10–31* (2001). Through her study of cultural parallels, Yoder concludes,

> *The evidence reveals a breadth of economic roles and responsibilities for royal and non-royal women. Women at Elephantine went about the market place buying, selling, and bartering various goods. At Dor, women engaged in a thriving textile industry. Some women assisted with the family business, managing properties, conducting transactions, and serving as parties to the purchase and sale*

*of slaves and land. Others made loans of cash and goods,
benefiting from favorable interest rates. Non-royal women
worked in a variety of professions at different ranks and
degrees of specialization. Shelomith, for example, had an
official capacity in the administrative affairs of Yehud. Other
women were supervisors . . . of workgroups, receiving generous
rations of grain, wine, and (occasionally) meat for their
efforts. There were also work forces composed predominantly
of women and children. . . . Royal women were renowned, in
particular, for their vast estates. They managed such properties
directly and through subordinates, authorizing transactions
with their own seals, ordering the movement of commodities,
employing and issuing rations to workers, and paying taxes
to the crown. They could also lease and sub-divide their
properties for profit. In short, "women's work" in the Persian
period was multifaceted and appears to have permeated all
sectors of the royal economy.* (113)

Yoder then sees that this articulation of the wise woman is linked to the
purposes of the creator God:

*It is her visage that elevates and theologically legitimates
women's activities as the embodiment of what it means to be
wise and a fearer of Yahweh.* (114)

Imagine that! A woman, out in public, embodying wisdom and reflective of faithful "fear of Yahweh"!

Yoder, however, is honest enough to recognize that, even in this
ode to a public woman, the woman characterized in the text is reflective of a male-dominated economy so that as a bride she remains a
commodity in a man's world. This woman, says Yoder, is at once "the
veneration and objectification of women's lives and work" (114). This is
about where Justice Alito leaves it, a woman venerated and objectified.

Such a reading indicates that in Proverbs 31, the work of emancipation of women is under way, but it surely is not completed.

Thus if we reach beyond such a suggestive text in Proverbs 31, we may arrive at the affirmation of Paul that some take to be a baptismal formula in the early church:

> *There is no longer Jew or Greek,*
> *there is no longer slave or free,*
> *there is no longer male or female,*
> *for all of you are one in Christ.* (Galatians 3:28)

Paul, in turn, takes up three of the most evident hierarchies in his world and sees that such hierarchies of value and power and privilege are overturned by the force of the gospel God. The power claimed by such hierarchies has no durable staying power in the world of the gospel. Thus the distinction of Jew and Greek that Paul had worked so hard to overcome. Thus the distinction of slave and free which Paul sees as overcome in the freedom of the gospel with its immense and continuing social implications. And thus concerning male and female, even though Paul hints elsewhere of his own continuing tilt toward then priority of males. Now, in the gospel, we can see that the world God intends is not ordered in terms of subordination or repression. Males have no priority or control over females, any more than masters who can no longer control slaves. The state, operated by men for men, has no right to control women's bodies.

The matter is made even more poignant when we notice that Brigitte Kahl (*Galatians Re-Imagined: Reading with the Eyes of the Vanquished* [2010]) has seen that "the law" that Paul resists in the letter to the Galatians is not the Jewish Torah (as it was taken to be in the old Lutheran formulation), but is the law of Rome, the law of the empire. It is exactly the law of the state, the one upon which Alito insists, that is rejected by Paul. It is time to "throw the book"—our Holy Book— against the lingering patriarchy that denies to women the capacity to live their own lives.

What we are witnessing in DC and in Kabul is the echo chamber of patriarchy. That patriarchy is long standing and seems very ordinary and normal. But seen in the light of the gospel of emancipation—about which Paul writes so compellingly—the claim of patriarchy is grotesque. It is as grotesque in DC as it is in Kabul. It echoes its own conviction of domination from DC to Kabul and back to DC. But it is being overthrown by the truth of the gospel. It is for good reason that Paul concludes his testimony in Galatians with an assertion of freedom:

> *For freedom Christ has set us free. Stand firm, therefore, and*
> *do not submit again to the yoke of slavery.* (Galatians 5:1)

Justice Alito and his comrades on the court aim to push back from freedom to the state rule of bondage. Alito and his comrades, of course, are well connected and well resourced so that, if and when necessary, they can secure "reproductive care" for their daughters and grand-daughters. They may indeed have moral compunction about abortion; there is no reason to doubt that. But along with that they have an eagerness to impose their particular moral compunctions on others who are subject to their ideological reasoning. Such an imposition does not ring true. What rings true is that the male-managed state wants, as in Kabul, to restrict the role of responsible freedom for women.

Paul in his ode to freedom in the gospel finishes his appeal by reference back to Sinai and, of all places, Leviticus:

> *For the whole law is summed up in a single commandment,*
> *"You shall love your neighbor as yourself."* (Galatians 5:14;
> see Leviticus 19:18)

How does one love one's self? How does a US Supreme Court justice love one's self? How does a leader of the Taliban love one's self? Obviously, expansive love of self is the capacity for self-care, self-management, and wellbeing. Subordination and repression are not acts of loving the neighbor. Subordination and repression are not and cannot be congruent with love of self or love of neighbor. The news is that the echo chamber of patriarchy has been thoroughly undermined and subverted by the God of emancipation. The force of God's will for self-determination by the neighbor is under way. It cannot be stopped, not even by the ideology-laden reasoning of the Court that is trapped in its own echo chamber.

ON GETTING US SOMETHING

You have heard that it was said, "An eye for an eye and a tooth for a tooth." But I say to you, Do not resist an evildoer. But if anyone strikes you on the right cheek, turn the other also; and if anyone wants to sue you and take your coat, give your cloak as well; and if anyone forces you to go one mile, go also the second mile. Give to everyone who begs from you, and do not refuse anyone who wants to borrow from you. (Matthew 5:38–42)

AS THE SERMON on the Mount (Matthew 5–7) constitutes the quintessence of Jesus's teaching, so this particular text articulates in most specific terms that his followers will bear the marks of second-mile forbearance in a new, very different life under the rule of God. Here is the most extreme and most demanding specificity of the radicality of the way of Jesus.

It is not surprising that this teaching has drawn the attention of the church. Luther specified that this mandate of Jesus pertained only to personal suffering. More daringly, Dietrich Bonhoeffer judged that "the distinction between person and office is wholly alien to the teaching of Jesus" (*The Cost of Discipleship* [1955], 123). He insists that the mandate applies to every sphere of life, including that of the public orbit. And of course Bonhoeffer's own life is an unmistakable living out of this mandate in the radical, costly decisions made by him.

This radical teaching has not only drawn attention among those who have sought the deep meaning of discipleship but also drawn the attention of those who mean to refute and resist his teaching—most notably Donald Trump, father and son. In an interview on April 14, 2016, Donald Trump (the father) was asked by Bob Lonsberry:

> *"Is there a favorite Bible verse or Bible story that has*
> *informed your thinking or your character through your life,*
> *sir?"*

As usual Trump does not hesitate to respond forcibly in his abundant, cynical ignorance. His answer promptly appealed to the Torah provisions of Exodus 21:23–24 (see also Leviticus 24:19–21):

> *If any harm follows, then you shall give life for life, eye for*
> *eye, tooth for tooth, hand for hand, foot for foot, burn for*
> *burn, wound for wound, stripe for stripe.*

Trump said:

> *Well, I think many. I mean, when we get into the Bible, I*
> *think many, so many. And some people, look, an eye for an*
> *eye, you see what's going on with our country, how people are*
> *taking advantage of us, and how they scoff at us and laugh*
> *at us. And they laugh at our face and they're taking our jobs,*
> *they're taking our money, they're taking the health of our*
> *country. And we have to be firm and have to be very strong.*
> *And we can learn a lot from the Bible, that I can tell you.*
> (Andrew Kaczynski, *BuzzFeed*, April 14, 2016)

Trump did not at all understand that this provision in the Torah aims to curb and restrain retaliation, or that it limits so that "not more than" can be taken in revenge than an eye or a tooth, or a hand, etc. Trump of course could not understand that, "tough guy" that he is, as his practice is to take, if he can, an arm and a leg for an eye. He would miss that retaliation has a limit. Nor would he have any notion of or interest in the fact that in his Sermon on the Mount Jesus has abrogated the law of retaliation by his teaching on submissiveness before evil.

Donald Jr. at least did a bit better than his father on the Bible. He at least knew about the counterteaching of Jesus. In his shamelessness Donald Jr. does not mind an easy dismissal of the teaching of Jesus. In a Turning Point USA conference last year, December 13 or so, he asserted:

> We've been playing tee-ball for half a century. While they're playing hardball and cheating. We've turned the other cheek, and I understand, sort of, the biblical reference. I understand the mentality. But it's gotten us nothing. OK? It's gotten us nothing while we've conceded ground in every major institution in our country.

His verdict, "Gotten us nothing," rings loud and true. His "sort of" indicates that he understands nothing at all of the teaching of Jesus. But he is right that the teaching of Jesus gets us nothing of power, nothing of wealth, nothing of control. Turning the other cheek has gotten us nothing! Then he added:

> And if we band together we can take on these institutions. That's where we've gone wrong for a long time. They cannot cancel us all. This will be contrary to a lot of our beliefs because I'd love not to have to participate in cancel culture. I'd love that it didn't exist. But as long as it does, folks, we better be playing the same game.

There can be no misperception of these specifications of father and son. The father believes the best part of the Bible is authorization of *revenge* and *retaliation*. The son believes the best part of life is to live in contradiction to the gospel because the way of power and aggression will "get us something" that the gospel denies us. We may be grateful that this pair of bold commentators, father and son, has made matters so clear for us. Donald Jr. sounds like a belated frantic echo of Nietzsche who readily dismissed Christian faith for its weakness. My college textbook on Nietzsche summarizes:

> *Christian meekness, forgiveness, patience, and love are no*
> *more than the mimicry of impotent hatred which dares not be*
> *anything but meek and patient, or seem anything but loving,*
> *though it dreams of heaven and hell.* (Frank Thilly and
> Ledger Wood, *A History of Philosophy* [1914/1951], 505)

I think there is very little value or mileage in spending time in responding to the Trump Doctrine, though I confess that their shameless declarations cause me to wonder where the many so-called evangelicals are, missing in action, when the teaching of Jesus is so blatantly contradicted and dismissed. In my estimate, we had better use our time for affirmative teaching and interpretation, not in refutation but in a patient positive exploration of the teaching of Jesus. Such teaching and interpretation is urgent among us because the deep claims of the gospel have been so much trivialized and compromised among us that his teaching goes almost unnoticed, and we go on unfazed. Thus in the face of such shameless cynicism that faithfully reflects the dominant modes of our culture, here is my proposal by way of response.

I suggest that pastors and congregations might take the time of the seven weeks of Lent soon coming upon us as a chance to walk around, in, and through this particular teaching of Jesus to see what discipleship might mean in a world of predatory capitalism and usurpatious white supremacy. The aim might be to show that *forgiveness* is the evangelical alternative to *revenge and retaliation*. The weeks might go like this:

1. The doxological affirmation of Israel that God is a God of generous, unreserved forgiveness:

The Lord is merciful and gracious,
slow to anger and abounding in steadfast love.
He will not always accuse, nor will he keep his anger forever.
He does not deal with us according to our sins,
nor repay us according to our iniquities. (Psalm 103:8–10)

2. The incomprehensible capacity of Jesus to forgive the empire in his moment of execution (Luke 23:34).
3. The bewilderment of his disciples at the forgiveness mathematics of Jesus (Matthew 18:21–22).
4. The economics of forgiveness as Jubilee (see Leviticus 25:13, 41; Isaiah 61:1–4; Luke 4:18–19).
5. The Lord's Prayer and the petition for forgiveness (Matthew 6:12; Luke 11:4), variously,

   Forgive us our debts as we forgive our debtors,
   Forgive our trespasses as we forgive those who trespass against us,
   Forgive us our sins as we forgive those who sin against us.

   In a capitalist society, many of us would rather have our *debts* forgiven than our *sins*!
6. The reconciling work of Desmond Tutu and the Truth and Reconciliation Commission in South Africa.
7. The indispensable work of reparations concerning the long-running "free labor" of slaves, on which see William A. Darity and A. Kristen Mullen, *From Here to Equality: Reparations for Black Americans in the Twenty-First Century* (2020).

Hannah Arendt, the great Jewish political philosopher, in her book *The Human Condition* (1958), asserts that the distinctive wonder of Christian faith is not the *resurrection* but *forgiveness*. We may linger to appreciate that bold observation. Of course it follows that after the seven weeks of Lent we Christians arrive at the joyous wonder of

Easter celebration in which we affirm that the power of death (in all its dangerous forms) will not and cannot prevail. Thus the "cheekiness" of Jesus teaching in our text is the prep work for Easter and the emergence of a new community of glad obedience in the world.

Ours is a dangerous and demanding time when hard decisions face us and we arrive at weighty either/or matters. For that reason our capacity to distinguish clearly between *the way of Christ* and *the way of the world* is urgent. It turns out that the way of Jesus has, to the contrary, "gotten us something." Where the gospel has been lived out, it continues to yield a life of neighborly wellbeing:

> . . . *they shall all sit under their own vines and under their*
>   *own fig trees,*
> *and no one shall make them afraid;*
> *for the mouth of the Lord of hosts has spoken.* (Micah 4:4)

❧ 19 ❧

THE ROLE OF GOVERNMENT?

Give the king our justice, O God,
and righteousness to a king's son.
May he judge your people with righteousness,
and your poor with justice.
May the mountains yield prosperity for the people,
and the hills, in righteousness.
May he defend the cause of the poor *of the people,*
give deliverance to the needy,
and crush the oppressor . . .
For he delivers the needy *when they call,*
the poor *and those who have no helper.*
He has pity on the weak *and* needy,
and saves the lives of the needy.
From oppression and violence he redeems their life;
and precious is their blood in his sight. (Psalm 72:1–4, 12–14)

IF YOU, DEAR reader, skipped over the biblical text cited above in order to get to this exposition, please go back and pay close attention to those verses. These remarkable verses are a part of a psalm that was likely read (or performed) at high occasions of royal liturgy. It is an articulation of the deepest claims of neighborly covenant to which the king (the government!) was answerable. If we notice the other verses of this psalm, it becomes clear that the prosperity, abundance, and well-being of the regime depended upon attentiveness to the most vulnerable neighbors. This claim intends to contradict any illusion the king might entertain that his prosperity and wellbeing depended otherwise upon the amassing of wealth, power, arms, or wisdom.

The point of the psalm is all the more poignant when it is recognized that the superscription to this psalm, tersely enough, is "of Solomon." This deliberate connection of Solomon to this psalm is an ironic acknowledgment that Solomon, of all the kings of ancient Israel, is the one who most counted on wealth, power, arms, and wisdom to sustain and assure his throne. Thus Solomon is narrated in the Bible as the most aggressively predatory of all of Israel's kings. And now, in the cadence of this liturgy, the king and his government are reminded that his rule is based on an unsubstantiated illusion. This intersection between this *stark liturgic claim* and *political reality* poses sharply for us, "What is the role of government?" The matter was of course in dispute in ancient Israel (see Deuteronomy 17:14–20; I Samuel 8:11–18); it continues among us to be in dispute. Is America "great again" because of its capacity for wealth, power, and wisdom (of which we have plenty), or is its greatness deeply linked to its attentiveness to our most vulnerable neighbors? This either/or is very deep in biblical faith, and is front and center in our current political economy.

I was led to think again about Psalm 72 because I have been reading *The Broken Constitution: Lincoln, Slavery, and the Refounding of America* by Noah Feldman (2021). The book concerns the complex, ambiguous relationship Abraham Lincoln had with the US Constitution as he slowly worked his way toward the Emancipation Proclamation. In short, Feldman's thesis is this:

- The original US Constitution was a compromised constitution, a compromise made with the South in order to voice an explicit sanction for the maintenance and continuation of slavery. The Constitution was compromised in that it lacked any moral sense about the matter. Lincoln initially judged that it was a

  > binding legal agreement deserving "reverence"
  > only insofar as it was based solely on "reason, cold,
  > calculating, unimpassioned reason." (316)

- Lincoln judged that the South, by its "rebellion" (secession), had broken that constitution. In response Lincoln felt ready to violate the Constitution in open and willing ways both by violating the right of *habeas corpus* and by suppression of newspapers. He judged such actions legitimate in light of the action of the South in breaking the Constitution.

- Slowly Lincoln worked his way to moral passion concerning slavery. His rhetoric built in the direction of moral passion culminating in the Gettysburg Address, wherein he could speak of a "new birth of freedom." That "new birth of freedom" came with the Emancipation Proclamation and the Thirteenth Amendment to the Constitution that resulted in a new moral, redeemed constitution. Thus concerning the "better angels" about which Lincoln spoke:

> *Put in terms of Lincoln's own political theology, the angels could easily be understood as the messengers who carried with them the truth of the new moral Constitution that followed from breaking the original Constitution of slavery.* (318)

Feldman's final statement is filled with both realism and hope:

> *Yet persistent inequality still exists in the United States, including inequality before the law, of the kind the moral Constitution prohibits. The reality is that the moral Constitution, like all constitutions, is not an end state but a promise of ongoing effort. Through the Constitution, we define our national project. But we never fully achieve it. Lincoln's legacy, then, is not the accomplishment of a genuinely moral Constitution. It is the breaking of the compromise Constitution—and the hope and promise of moral Constitution that will always be in the process of being redeemed.* (327)

It is sobering and hope-filled to read about the evolution of Lincoln's thought and action in light of the royal mandate of Psalm 72. That psalm assigns to the government responsibility for redress of injustice, exactly the kind of redress that Lincoln finally undertook. It is no wonder that Lincoln's presidential actions are freighted with sobriety and solemnity because the redress of injustice is difficult and dangerous work. The psalm leaves us in no doubt about the urgency of the matter. Lincoln, moreover, understood that moral urgency only gradually, cautiously, and slowly. He did not in the end, however, waver from the hard work that properly belonged to his governance. As Doris Kearns Goodwin has seen, Lincoln knew with remarkable awareness the combination of *transformative vision* and *transactional shrewdness* that was indispensable to good governance. His work brings about the redress of a shame-filled compromise. Feldman is surely correct that that hard work remains for us unfinished. For all of his deliberate slowness, Lincoln caught the main claim of the psalm; he made the government over which he presided an agent of redress.

The unambiguous conclusion of Psalm 72 and the wise analysis of Feldman were together fresh in my mind as I watched and listened to the recent hearing by the Supreme Court of the Mississippi law that would preclude all abortions. It occurred to me that the arguments in support of the Mississippi law and the evident tilt of too many of the "Justices" were not unlike a replay of the old arguments in defense of slavery. In the hearing,

On exhibit was the old compromised, broken Constitution;

On exhibit was the continuing force of white patriarchy that aims to keep all "others" securely "under control";

On exhibit was the readiness of too many of the "Justices" to settle for the new title "Injustice," as in "Injustice Alito," "Injustice Thomas," etc.

On exhibit was the pernicious readiness of the court to operate in terms of "reason, cold, calculating, unimpassioned reason" without reference to real people on whom their ruling would impinge in severe ways. (See the discerning assessment of this perniciousness by Linda Greenhouse, "The Supreme Court Gaslights Its Way to the End of Roe," *New York Times*, December 4, 2021, A19.)

On exhibit was the ludicrous reasoning of "Justice" Barrett with her easy reassuring concern for carrying a baby to term and dropping it off at the mother's convenience.

On exhibit was the reckless cynicism of "Justice" Cavanaugh who advocated "neutrality" by the court, who asked, "Why should this court be the arbiter?" Why indeed? What might be the purpose of such courage on the part of the court? Or what might be the service rendered by neutrality to white patriarchy? (Already in Deuteronomy 17:8–13 Moses could imagine a supreme court that could and would decide hard cases!)

On exhibit was the power of government mobilized with indifference toward the subjects of Psalm 72—the poor, the needy, and the oppressed. Such subjects of the law could not appear on the screen of the "Justices" who were committed to the abiding claims of white patriarchy.

What was not on exhibit in the hearing (with some important exceptions) was much moral passion for the needy, the poor, or the oppressed who are surely victims of male predation and surely the targets of the Mississippi law. In the place of such moral passion there was cold calculating, unimpassioned reason. The outcome of the hearing raises the urgent questions: From where could come moral passion on this issue that is something other than simply knee-jerk advocacy on behalf of the unnamed, uncared for unborn? From where will come moral passion concerning the systemic neglect of those sisterly bodies who must bear the brunt of such unnoticing advocacy? Thus far the moral issue of respect and regard for the freedom of the bodies of women has mostly been carried by secularists who make constitutional arguments. But moral passion goes beneath and beyond constitutional questions. It concerns real people, their bodies, their suffering, and their futures. Such moral passion that this issue merits must eventually come from the religious community that is in solidarity with "widows, orphans, and immigrants" and that has a stake in the future and wellbeing of victimized young women and exploited young girls who are not mere containers for the unborn workforce.

For good reason Feldman has concluded that the Constitution is still "in process of being redeemed." It is settled lore among us that those who have the most prefer a minimal government, whereas those in deep need inescapably hope for an activist government of effective redress. For good reason, against the massive force of money, power, and wisdom, the psalm reminds us of the nonnegotiable condition of communal prosperity and abundance.

In his speech, "How Long, Not Long" in Montgomery on March 25, 1965, Martin Luther King Jr. concluded with this ringing affirmation:

> *I know you are asking today, "How long will it take?"*
> *Somebody's asking "How long will prejudice blind the visions*
> *of men, darken their understanding, and drive bright-eyed*
> *wisdom from her sacred throne?" Somebody's asking, "When*
> *will wounded justice, lying prostrate on the streets of Selma*
> *and Birmingham and communities all over the South, be*
> *lifted from this dust of shame to reign supreme among the*
> *children of men?" . . . "How long will justice be crucified,*
> *and truth bear it?" I come to say to you this afternoon,*
> *however difficult the moment, however frustrating the hour,*
> *it will not be long, because "truth crushed to earth will rise*
> *again." How long? Not long, because "no lie can live forever."*
> *How long? Not long, because "you shall reap what you sow."*

King's question persists along with Feldman's verdict about being in the process of being redeemed. The question is "How long?"

Not long indeed before *the Constitution of Compromise* becomes *the Redeemed Restored Constitution of American justice.* It is "not long" indeed before the moral reality of the poor, the needy, and the oppressed is fully recognized among us. It will not be long after the courage and imagination of moral urgency are mobilized among us.

20

THE SIZE OF GOVERNMENT:
A RETRACTION

WELL, THIS IS not really a *retraction* but a further *exploration*. In a recent exposition entitled, "The Role of Government?" I reiterated a truism of common assumption:

> *It is settled lore among us that those who have the most*
> *prefer a minimal government, whereas those in deep need*
> *inescapably hope for an activist government of effective*
> *redress.*

I am glad to retract that truism. That truism, albeit from a simpler time, reflects the "small government" notion of Thomas Jefferson, a sentiment well articulated by Henry David Thoreau: "The government is best which governs least" (*Civil Disobedience* [1849]). That claim has become a favorite mantra for market ideology that wants mightily to resist government regulation, as "the government" was seen or projected as hostile to market forces. And even Bill Clinton, amid his presidency, loudly exclaimed that "The era of big government is over." Except, of course, President Clinton did not mean that; he continued to thrive on big government. He meant only that he would shrink government welfare support for needy people, while the rest of government continued to prosper and expand.

In fact very few people would actually choose small government. Even a Republican farmer is glad for government support of prices for his crops. Even "red states" welcome federal aid in cases of emergency. And even a small town businessperson is glad to receive a bailout from the government from the slump caused by the COVID-19 virus. Thus "small government" is a convenient ideological mantra that is not to be taken with any seriousness because, in a variety of ways, almost everyone counts on government support and sustenance.

I was illuminated on this line of thinking by the rich work of Loïc Wacquant, a sociologist in Berkeley. In his book, *Punishing the Poor: The Neoliberal Government of Social Insecurity* (2009), and in his subsequent article, "Crafting the Neoliberal State: Workfare, Prisonfare, and Social Insecurity" (*Sociological Forum* 25, no. 2 [2010]: 197–220), Wacquant exposes the ways in which market forces no longer oppose the government but in fact now occupy the government and bend it to its own purposes. The result is government expansion in obedience to the needs and wants of market interests, that is, in response to those who benefit most from the expansion of such governance. We now have "big government" in the service of such forces, thus "The Growth of the Neoliberal State." "Small government" is a convenient and compelling mantra that functions to conceal the sociopolitical realities of our public situation that is of crisis proportions.

Wacquant nicely identifies the "left hand" of the state as the "feminine side of Leviathan" that is marked by "spendthrift" notions in the form of public education, health, housing, welfare, and labor law that function to "offer protection and succor to those categories shorn of economic and cultural capital" (201). The "right hand," conversely the masculine side, imposes economic discipline "via budget cuts, fiscal incentives, and economic deregulation." Or to change the imagery slightly, there is now transition from the kindly "nanny state" to the strict "daddy state" of neoliberalism. (This page in Wacquant has to be one of the most remarkable and moving pages I have read in a very long time!)

There is nothing "small" or "limited" about the masculine "daddy state" of neoliberalism. We may attend particularly to the fierce expansiveness of the state in its incarceration of the poor and the economically vulnerable and disabled. With his gift for phrasing, Wacquant can observe:

> *The misery of American welfare and the grandeur of*
> *American prisonfare at century's turn are the two sides of the*
> *same political coin. The generosity of the latter is in direct*
> *proportion to the stinginess of the former, and it expands to*
> *the degree that both are driven by moral behaviorism.* (203)

What an eye-catcher: "The grandeur of American prisonfare"! Or in another such phrasing, Wacquant writes of "*rolling back*" the social safety net and the "*rolling out*" of the police-and-prison dragnet that specializes in the "development of short-term contracts, temporary jobs, and underpaid traineeships, and expansion of the latitude of employers in hiring, firing and the use of overtime" (210) (italics added).

If we were to seek an analogue in the Bible for such an expansive state, we would look to the narrative of King Solomon (on which see my book, *Solomon: Israel's Ironic Icon of Human Achievement* [2005]). It is reported that Solomon developed a vigorous tax-collecting system (I Kings 4:7–19), that he and his royal entourage ate lavishly amid a peasant economy (I Kings 4:22–23), that he controlled the forced labor of 30,000 Israelites (I Kings 5:13), that he had access to acres and acres of gold (I Kings 6:20–22, 7:48–50), that he had a sizable arsenal of horses and chariots (I Kings 9:15–19,10:26–29), and that he easily belonged with the global power elite (see I Kings 10:1–10). We know, moreover, that Solomon's regime ended in a disaster (I Kings 12:1–19). It was a regime vigorously opposed by the prophets who voiced the covenantal alternative of Israel's tradition (see the prophet Ahijah in I Kings 12:29–39). We should not make too much of this analogue of Solomon and the neoliberal state because Solomon lacked the mechanisms of the contemporary neoliberal enterprise. Nonetheless, *the drive of anxious greed* and *the outcome of disastrous injustice* are exactly the same in the two cases. Solomon presided over a "daddy state" that imposed severe and uncompromising discipline on vulnerable peasants.

Wacquant concludes that the new global ruling class relies on the "close articulation of four institutional logics" (213):

1. Economic deregulation in order to promote "the market."
2. Welfare state devolution, retraction, and recomposition along with support for the intensification of commodification. This is expressed in policies of "workfare."
3. An expansive, intrusive, and proactive penal apparatus.
4. The cultural trope of individual responsibility so that the super-rich can imagine they are self-made and so that the economic victims of greed can be blamed for their condition.

Clearly the size of government is now a nonissue. Indeed the neoliberal state can easily accept the claim that "big is better," bigger impositions of workfare, bigger prison populations, and bigger ego claims by the "successful."

The issue of "big government" or "small government" is thus rendered among us as a phony issue. The deep and abidingly urgent issue is not *the size of government* but *the role of government*. So we are back to Psalm 72, and the plight of the poor, the needy, and the oppressed who suffer at the hands of violent systemic injustice imposed by the neoliberal state. Neoliberal ideology intends that government should serve the aims and ends of individualized wealth at the expense of the vulnerable labor market. (It is for that reason that Starbucks and Amazon go to great lengths to resist the formation of labor unions.) The counter to this predation is not really "left hand" or "feminization," though these may be useful images. The real issue is restorative justice:

> *Justice, and only justice, you shall pursue, so that you may*
> *live and occupy the land that the Lord your God is giving*
> *you.* (Deuteronomy 16:20)

The violation of this mandate of the Torah is shared in the predation of Solomon and in the predation by the neoliberal state. Thus to
reiterate:

> *Give the king your justice, O God,*
> *and your righteousness to a king's son.*
> *May he judge your people with righteousness,*
> *and your poor with justice.*
> *May the mountains yield prosperity for the people,*
> *and the hills righteousness.*
> *May he defend the cause of the poor of the people,*
> *give deliverance to the needy,*
> *and crush the oppressor . . .*
> *For he delivers the needy when they call,*
> *the poor and those who have no helper.*
> *He has pity on the weak and the needy,*
> *and saves the lives of the needy.*
> *From oppression and violence he redeems their life;*
> *and precious is their blood in his sight.* (Psalm 72:1–4, 12–14)

As I thought about *the size of government* in relation to *the role of
government*, I remembered the anticipatory oracle of Isaiah to which
we Christians appeal at Christmas. The prophet anticipates the coming
of the "good king" (messiah) who will undertake the proper role of
government. The birth announcement (or perhaps the coronation
liturgy) of the new king gives the king elaborate royal titles (see my
little book, *Names for the Messiah*):

> *For a child has been born for us,*
> *a son given to us;*
> *authority rests upon his shoulders;*
> *and he is named Wonderful Counselor, Mighty God,*
> *Everlasting Father, Prince of Peace.* (Isaiah 9:6)

The new government will have many roles: counselor, military might, peace. And then this:

> *His* authority shall grow continually
> *and there shall be endless peace*
> *for the throne of David and his kingdom.*
> *He will establish and uphold it with justice and with*
>   *righteousness*
> *from this time onward and forevermore.*
> *The zeal of the Lord of hosts will do this.* (Isaiah 9:7)

The NRSV translates, "his authority will grow." The more familiar KJV has it:

> *The* increase of his government *shall know no end.*

Talk about "big government"! The prophet anticipates that the rule of the new coming Davidic king will be expansive, whether in authority or in territory. If the oracle initially pertained to King Hezekiah, then the prospect is the recovery of northern territory from the Assyrians. Beyond territorial recovery, however, the prophet anticipates the *growing governance of justice and righteousness*, that is, the expansiveness of neighborly solidarity and community wellbeing.

The growth and increase of *God's governance of justice and righteousness* surely constitute the substance of the initial announcement of Jesus, "The Kingdom of God is at hand" (Mark 1:15). "At hand" is the rule of justice and righteousness. "At hand" is the governance that is embodied in the restorative ministry of Jesus:

> *The blind received their sight, the lame walk, the lepers are*
> *cleansed, the deaf hear, the dead are raised, the poor have*
> *good news brought to them.* (Luke 7:22)

This is the burden of the new governance that Isaiah anticipated. This is the governance that is entrusted peculiarly to the church. It is this governance for which the church advocates in the public domain. It follows that the church is all for "big government" of a certain kind. It follows that the church must join issue with the oppressive expansiveness of the neoliberal state:

1. To join issue with economic deregulation by serious regulation of predatory economic forces;
2. To join issue with workfare state requirements by insisting that the state is a tool of the community for the assurance of wellbeing for all of its members;
3. To join issue with an "expansive, intrusive, proactive penal apparatus" by advocacy for serious insistence upon rehabilitation that aims at the ending of incarceration of the defenseless. Not without reason did the eruption of the gospel have prisons in purview:

   > *He has sent me to bring good news to the oppressed,*
   > *to bind up the brokenhearted,*
   > *to proclaim liberty to the captives,*
   > *and* release to the prisoners. (Isaiah 61:1; see Luke 4:18–19)

4. To join issue with the trope of individual responsibility by an insistence upon community solidarity through the maintenance of stable viable public institutions.

A prophetic insistence on the justice and righteousness of God exposes the phoniness and illusion of government *of* the powerful, *for* the wealthy, *by* the well-connected. The covenantal-prophetic tradition always and everywhere joins issue with the seductions that feed the neoliberal state. Our textual tradition is loaded with *sharp critiques* of those seductions and with *emancipated alternatives* to those seductions.

In the gospel narratives "Solomon" is on the lips of Jesus only twice. In the Sermon on the Mount, Jesus observes of the birds and flowers that "not even Solomon" had as much splendor and glory

(Matthew 6:29; Luke 12:127). And in Matthew 12:42 and Luke 11:31, Jesus declares of his movement that "something greater than Solomon is here." In both instances, Jesus dismisses the importance or impressiveness of Solomon:

> *Not even Solomon . . .*
> *Something greater than Solomon . . .*

The predatory wealth of Solomon is contrasted with the wonder of the new governance that is without anxiety. The new governance concerns a radical reordering of priorities, away from greed, wealth, power, and leverage.

In the Christian tradition Christmas is the rebirth of the new governance. It is no wonder that the angels sang of new governance; it is no wonder that shepherds were amazed at the new governance. It is no wonder that the wisest of men knelt before the new governance. And then there is a direct line to Good Friday because Pharaoh–Caesar–Herod will not and cannot ever easily settle amid the new governance (see Matthew 2:16–18). Christmas stirs and heats up the long-running dispute between regimes of anxious greed and the new governance. The church is an active player in that ongoing dispute. The church does not believe "there are good people on both sides." More than that, the church believes that the will and purpose of the God of justice and righteousness, mercy, compassion, and steadfast love will prevail. It will prevail in the face of the mighty predatory power of a different "big government." Imagine: the church as an active party to that deep contention! There is no doubt about the matter in the great liturgical cadences of the church:

> *Unto us a child is born,*
> > *who bears the titles of justice and righteousness,*
> > > *whose authority and governance will grow and*
> > > > *increase . . .*
> > > *soon and soon!*

Part IV

WAR AND PEACE

21

IRON RATIONED

Now there was no smith to be found throughout all the land of Israel; for the Philistines said, "The Hebrews must not make swords or spears for themselves"; so all the Israelites went down to the Philistines to sharpen their plowshare, mattocks, axes or sickles; the charge was two-thirds of a shekel for the plowshares and for the mattocks, and one-third for sharpening the axes and for setting the goads. (I Samuel 13:19–21)

THIS BRIEF, INNOCENT looking text is one never heard in church. It nonetheless tells us a great deal about the socioeconomic and military situation of Israel in the early days of Israel's settlement in the land. We know from the several narratives that the Philistines were Israel's great nemesis in those early days. Thus Saul fought against the Philistines (I Samuel 13:1–7), Jonathan routed the Philistines (14:1–24), David confronted and defeated the Philistine "champion" (I Samuel 17:1–54), Saul rescued the town of Keilah from the Philistines (23:1–14), and eventually the Philistines killed Saul and Jonathan (I Samuel 31:1–10).

We know that the Philistines were part of the movement of the "Sea Peoples," a migration that swept south and west at the beginning of the Iron Age. (I am happy to report that my first paper in graduate school was a paper on "The Sea Peoples" under George Landis.) The Philistines, in Israelite perspective, represented a very different culture, a difference marked in Israelite lore by tagging them as "uncircumcised" (I Samuel 14:6, 17:26, 36, 31:4; II Samuel 1:20). They constituted a powerful continuing competitor to Israel for control of the land of the

Shephelah on the southwest edge of "Palestine." The Philistine's threat to Israel did not subside until David's decisive victory in the Valley of Rephaim (II Samuel 5:17–25).

In our text we have a report on an instance in the ongoing struggle of these two peoples who vied for control of the land. In this instance the Philistines had the upper hand and were determined to keep it so. One way of maintaining dominance by the Philistines over Israel was to deny Israel access to the equipment required to flourish. Thus it is reported that the Philistines did not allow the Israelites to have any blacksmiths in Israel, that is, any artisan who could work with and shape iron into useful tools. As a result, Israel could not produce for themselves the tools needed for agriculture . . . no plowshares, no axes, no sickles, and no pickaxes (mattocks). The Israelites had to rely on production of such tools by the Philistine blacksmiths so that the Philistines could control production and so limit Israel's capacity for agriculture. That in itself may have been an impediment to economic prosperity for the agricultural community. But of course the greater danger for the Philistines, noted in the text, is that an Israelite blacksmith could readily take iron intended for agricultural use and reshape such iron for weapons of war. Thus the Philistine prohibition on blacksmiths in Israel amounts to arms control and the inability of Israel to maintain military equipment to protect itself from an attack by the Philistines. We are told, moreover, that when an Israelite necessarily engaged a Philistine blacksmith, the fees were quite high. Thus on all counts Israel was kept dependent and therefore vulnerable, without means for the growth of its agricultural economy and without military capacity.

The capacity of the Philistines to limit and control iron (and therefore weapons) was on my mind as I thought about gun violence in the United States and the recent decision of the Supreme Court to make guns everywhere more available. The Court's decision in *The District of Columbia v. Heller* in 2008 made guns widely available in a way that has led to an explosion of gun violence. In seeking to understand the Second Amendment and that Court decision, I have been informed by Thom Hartmann, *The Hidden History of Guns and the Second Amendment* (2019), who was in turn informed by Carl Bogus's "The Hidden History of the Second Amendment" (*UC Davis Law Review* 31 [1998]: 309). Hartmann, after Bogus, shows that behind the amendment was the long history of slave state "militia" whose work was to patrol and control slaves and to recover escaped slaves. The leaders of the plantation economy (e.g., Jefferson, Madison) feared a standing army, and would have none of it. One reason for resistance to a standing army was that any slave who served in the army would have a claim to emancipation. Such leaders did not want such an army, but wanted instead to assure that the reach of the federal government would not and could not do away with "state militia." Thus the amendment guarantees the continuing right of such "organized militia" to work their unrestrained will in the slave economy, unhindered by federal check or restraint. The purpose of the amendment was to continue the means to control the slave population. The only ones who could rightly have a gun had to be a "citizen," which of course meant a white property owner. Thus guns were safely withheld from any slave (or any Black) person, none of whom could qualify as a citizen. Thus Hartman can conclude:

> *It didn't take any time at all for white southerners to realize that if the race-based hierarchy of the Old South was to be preserved, white people needed to be the only armed people. . . . Today the genocide of Native Americans has settled into a slow simmer of malnutrition, poverty, and voter suppression; the enslavement of people of African descent has shifted from plantations to slums and prisons; and the modern police state constructed during the conquest era, the slavery era, and Reconstruction after the Civil War, and thrown into high gear in the 1970s with Nixon's war on drugs, is still alive and well. All it requires to keep it in place is lots of guns.* (65, 89)

The Philistines would have followed the calculus of this reasoning with appreciative judgment!

The ruling of the Court in the Heller case that made guns widely available turned out to be one of the worst Supreme Court decisions, and one of the most poorly reasoned of any decision. Justice Scalia, who wrote the majority opinion, had made for himself a reputation as an "originalist." It is clear, however, that he has no claim to be an originalist in this case, for in this opinion he devised an entirely new justification for guns to protect "hearth and home"; he gave reason for his judgment that had never been before the Court. No court heretofore had thought that the amendment concerned a private right to guns. The outcome of that opinion has been the fostering of new gun usage and, consequently, an eruption of violence in many social settings. Hartmann observes of much of recent gun violence (87):

1. The shooter is characteristically white and male,
2. The shooter kills indiscriminately in response to a strongly felt grievance, and
3. The shooter's actions are "strangely explained away" as a "lone wolf," or mental disturbance.

Thus much of the gun violence continues to be in the hands of whites in a new gun culture that is without restraint or check. While the Philistines had a policy of keeping "iron" out of the hands of Israelites, our current polices have been surfeit of guns in the hands of whites in a continuing assault on Blacks by unrestrained police and other militia groups.

The Philistines feared that the Israelites would beat their plowshares, mattocks, axes, and sickles into swords and spears. They understood that iron is readily converted from *agricultural tools* into *weapons of war*. What the Philistines did not anticipate was that there would arise in Israel poets who had the remarkable vision of doing conversion in the opposite direction, from weapons of war to agricultural tools:

They shall beat their swords into plowshares,
and their spears into pruning hooks;
nation shall not lift up sword against nation,
neither shall they learn war any more. (Isaiah 2:4; Micah 4:3)

It is a stunning act of prophetic imagination to propose that society does not need to be ordered according to lethal weapons, not according to guns made regularly and everywhere available, not according to guns assigned to "well organized militia," not according to guns used to monitor, control, or intimidate vulnerable populations. Of course the Philistines could observe the eagerness of Israelites, via Saul, Jonathan, and David, to convert their tools into weapons. The Philistines did not know of the counterview of the poets and surely could not have trusted that vision in any case.

More likely the Philistines would themselves have gravitated to the conversion of *tools to weapons* urged by the prophet Joel who counters his poetic antecedents:

Beat your plowshares into swords,
and your pruning hooks into spears;
let the weakling say, "I am a warrior." (Joel 3:10;
     Hebrews 4:10)

Joel's poetic imperative is situated in a summons to war that has overtones of apocalyptic urgency: "for the day of the Lord is near in the valley of decision" (v. 14). But then, such apocalyptic urgency is always on the lips of those who are filled with fear and anger and who imagine that war or some such armed violence is a necessary and adequate solution to the issue at hand. Joel's fearful summons is the more popular response to crisis, and he could see the danger all around. Joel judged, as we often do, that the forceful use of "iron" will assure security. Thus in Israel we have two competing, contradictory poetic scenarios. On the one hand, Isaiah and Micah, in the more familiar poetry, imagine a move *from weapons to tools*. Joel, in a less well-known scenario, summons *from tools to weapons*.

We may judge that the move *from tools to weapons* is based in *fear*, perhaps even fear that is warranted. Conversely, the move *from weapons to tools* is based in *hope* that "not learning war" will lead to more beneficial social outcomes. If we juxtapose the two poetic offers, we can see that the issue is one of fear versus hope. And admittedly, hope seems fragile and flimsy in the face of real threat.

Likely the Philistines would not know how to respond to such an either/or, bound as they were to the practice of weapons and the force of war. And so it is in much of our world. The remarkable claim of biblical poetry is that the other alternative of hope is kept alive on the lips of the poets. In the end, the community of faith bets on hope and refuses to succumb to the force of fear that is all around. The contest of fear and hope, of "tools to weapons" or "weapons to tools" is currently as alive for us as it always is.

We may note that in our passage from I Samuel 13, the narrative reports in the last sentence that the way in which the Philistines had rationed iron to Israel had worked:

> *So on the day of the battle neither sword nor spear was to be found in the possession of any of the people with Saul and Jonathan.* (v. 22)

But then, quite remarkably, there is this laconic note at the end:

> *But Saul and his son Jonathan had them.* (v. 22)

The narrative offers no explanation. We are left to wonder; had they a secret deal with the Philistines? Or had they a surreptitious blacksmith?

Or are we to think the Lord of Hosts had armed them? In any case, we learn that the rationing of iron by the Philistines is not foolproof; it never is and never can be! Iron may be rationed by the strong and kept from the vulnerable; however the iron is distributed, we are left with fear . . . or with hope! *Hope outruns fear* in the same way that *tools* eventually will *outrun weapons*!

22

ON THE WAY TO
PEACEABLE TORAH

THERE IS, IN Israel's prophetic tradition, a strong appreciation for Jerusalem as the epicenter of the world. The ancient city of Jerusalem features the seat of Davidic governance and the temple where God is known to dwell. Concerning the Jerusalem temple as the place of divine habitation, the psalms make exuberant affirmation.

> *There is a river whose streams make glad the city of God,*
> *the holy habitation of the Most High.*
> *God is in the midst of the city;*
> *it shall not be moved;*
> *God will help it when the morning dawns.* (Psalm 46:4–5)

> *We ponder your steadfast love, O God,*
> *in the midst of your temple.*
> *Your name, O God, like your praise,*
> *reaches to the ends of the earth.*
> *Your right hand is filled with victory.* (Psalm 48:9–10)

Indeed Psalm 48:14 is nicely ambiguous in its exclamation: "This is our God." The reference is to the God who inhabits the temple. But the grammar permits "this" to be the temple itself, as though the temple itself were the bodily articulation of God's presence. That same high view of the city is reiterated by Isaiah in the midst of the Assyrian threat. Only for Isaiah, the central point is that Jerusalem will be saved because it is the seat of the Davidic establishment:

> *For I will defend this city to save it, for my own sake and for*
> *the sake of my servant David.* (Isaiah 37:35)

Both monarchy and temple, royal presence and divine presence, make Jerusalem the peculiar accent point of Israel's affirmation and affection.

In the most familiar prophetic texts, however, the accent on Jerusalem is very different. In a poem shared by Isaiah (2:2–4) and Micah (Micah 4:1–4), the city matters because it is the habitat of Israel's Torah. In the tradition the Torah has been transferred from its origin at Sinai to its locus in Jerusalem. The move of the Torah from Sinai to Zion causes Torah instruction, assigned at Sinai to Israel, to become global and universal in its reach from Jerusalem. Thus the poets can imagine a scenario in which all the nations will willingly and eagerly join in a procession to Jerusalem.

> *Many peoples shall come and say,*
> *"Come, let us go up to the mountain of the Lord,*
> *to the house of the God of Jacob;*
> *that he may teach us his ways*
> *and that we may walk in his paths."*
> *For out or Zion shall go forth instruction,*
> *and the word of the Lord from Jerusalem.* (Isaiah 2:3;
>   Micah 4:2)

The purpose of the procession is that all nations may receive instruction from "the word of the Lord." The Torah teaching pertains to all nations. Specifically, the Torah teaching will lead to a sober, just adjudication of disputes among the nations; the teaching, moreover, will result in disarmament. Because the Torah teaches and urges both "love of God" and "love of neighbor," it is a reliable guide for peaceable coexistence among the nations, a peaceableness that makes war unproductive and useless. (Or as Jesus later summarizes "the weightier matters" of the Torah: justice, mercy, and faith [Matthew 23:23].)

Consequently, the prophets can readily imagine that the nations of the world will gladly disarm and turn their inventory of arms into the production of useful agricultural equipment. The task to be done will be the transformation of swords, spears, bombs, and missiles and the new production will be plowshares and pruning hooks. All of this from the epicenter of moral instruction from Israel's Jerusalem Torah.

While the two prophets share this anticipatory poetry, Micah, an agricultural peasant, adds a verse of rural realism that is not included in the Isaiah articulation of the poem:

> *But they shall all sit under their own vines and under their own*
> *fig trees,*
> *and no one shall make them afraid;*
> *for the mouth of the Lord of hosts has spoken.* (Micah 4:4)

The outcome of disarmament will be to a modest rural economy in which peaceable people will enjoy a vine and a fig tree that is not under threat. This modest promise of food may be more fully appreciated when it is contrasted with the extravagant royal menu of King Solomon that could only be sustained by aggressive militarism:

> *Solomon's provision for one day was thirty cors of choice flour,*
> *and sixty cors of meal, ten fat oxen, and twenty pasture fed*
> *cattle, one hundred sheep, besides deer, gazelles, roebucks, and*
> *fatted fowl.* (I Kings 4:22)

A diet of rich extravagant meat requires aggressive arms in order to monopolize food in such a way. The prophet Micah knew that economic and military choices were to be made. For the prophet the either/or is not complicated. Either *a rich diet of much meat with swords and spears*; or *a modest diet of figs and grapes with pruning hooks and plowshares*. It is a clear, unambiguous choice, and the prophets are left with no doubt about which choice Israel must make. This Torah teaching makes Jerusalem the moral epicenter of international life and makes Torah the great teacher of all the nations in the way of peace. The prophetic tradition proceeds on the assumption that this demanding teaching is without parallel anywhere other than in the Torah.

We should notice that the prophet Ezekiel voices a very high view of Jerusalem as the epicenter of the world, though his imagery is in a very different mode from that of Isaiah and Micah. Ezekiel has God assert of Jerusalem:

> *I have set her in* the center of the nations, *with countries all around her.* (5:5)

That assertion of Jerusalem's centrality to the international community, however, is made only so that Ezekiel can declare the moral failure of the city in what follows. It is likely that the imagery of the tree in 7:22–24 and 31:8–9 also bespeaks Jerusalem as the epicenter of creation. Most important, in 38:12, Ezekiel can write of the "center of the earth" where the nations may gather to plunder. Ezekiel's interest in architectural geography leads in a distinctively different direction from that of Isaiah and Micah. Our discussion remains focused on these two prophets and their shared vision of a Jerusalem Torah that can teach the nations. This teaching, taken in Israel to be without parallel, makes Jerusalem the moral center of international life and the great teacher of all the nations of the world.

In the New Testament in at least one instance Jesus deconstructs the claim of Jerusalem in his declaration to the "Samaritan women":

> *The hour is coming when you will worship the Father neither on this mountain* [Samaria] *nor Jerusalem. . . . But the hour is coming, and is now here, when the true worshipper will worship the Father in spirit and truth, for the Father seeks such as these to worship him.* (John 4:21–23)

The defining mark of "in spirit and truth" is a refusal of any geographical claim and instead an embrace of a claim of covenantal substance.

I was pondering this prophetic image of an international procession to Jerusalem for the sake of instruction and disarmament when I read *The Chancellor: The Remarkable Odyssey of Angela Merkel* by Katie Marton (2021). The book is an appreciative but critical biography of Angela Merkel, who led the German government from 2005 to 2021. The book traced Merkel's rapid rise to power, her unblinking response to President Putin, her disdain for President Trump, and her courage in dealing with President Xi. The book stresses the importance of Merkel's deliberate pace of leadership, her refusal to engage in emotive rhetoric, her resistance to tribal defensiveness, and her wise courage for policies that were not always popular. Most specifically in the European crisis of 2015 refugees from Syria flooded into Europe and eventually into Germany. Merkel invited many thousands of refugees into Germany. Marton makes it clear, moreover, that while Merkel's policy was dangerous and daring in admitting many thousands of refugees into Germany, she also took care to nurture public opinion toward willing hospitality. Her policy in general met with approval from her voters. Thus she proceeded with wise prudence. Merkel herself never wavered in her conviction that such a welcome to refugees was the right thing to do as she boldly asserted, "Wir schaffen das," that is, "We can do this." She did it! She risked a great deal and was wondrously vindicated in her bold leadership.

It turns out that the refugee crisis was definitive for Merkel in her courage and moral sensibility. But her decision-making in that crisis was not atypical for her. As a result of her durable policies, her unflappability, her sober judgment, and her human realism, she eventually emerged as the leader of Europe. Marton yields this judgment of her:

> *Nothing short of astonishing is that the country responsible*
> *for the Holocaust is now regarded as the world's moral center.*
> (300)

Imagine at the beginning of our most vexed twenty-first century that faces the rising authoritarianism of Putin in Russia and Xi in China, and the embarrassment of Trump in the United States and the white supremacy that he advocates . . . imagine to be able to generate a "moral center." I do not want to overstate the point, but Merkel's leadership in Germany has made her a moral instructor not unlike the Jerusalem anticipated by the prophets, a point of reference to which other nations may go for guidance and resources. Given Germany's postwar aversion to militarism, an aversion gladly embraced by Merkel, perhaps Germany provides a vision to which other nations may go to learn peacemaking as a preference to war-making. If the nations learn that much, we will have Merkel's good judgment and sober courage to thank. The centrality of Germany via Merkel is caught in a quip from Henry Kissinger. He was asked for the phone number of Europe. He answered, "Call Merkel." Indeed! Without underplaying Merkel's practical political sense, given her Lutheran rootage, we may appreciate the extent to which she has governed "in spirit and truth." We may learn from Merkel's leadership that the "moral leadership of the world" can and will relocate to wherever "spirit and truth" are practiced.

As I thought about this prophetic vision of all the nations streaming in procession to Jerusalem for instruction in justice and peace, and as I thought about Merkel's leadership that made her an unwavering moral center, I also thought of the destiny and current addictive pathologies of the United States. I can remember back in the quaint days of Eisenhower that we could say, without blush or embarrassment, that the United States was "the leader of the free world." We were not quite "the moral center," but we came relatively close to such a claim. But now the United States is not a "leader" in any way that counts and certainly not a "moral center." Oh, wait! Yes, we are world leader in a couple of claims:

- We are the world leader in *civic violence* through which our children and our institutions are under violent threat.

- We are the world leader in *violent white supremacy*, for that, after all, is what Trump and the moral failure of the Republican Party is all about. And that urgent aggressive force will not stop until whites claim the field of power and influence.

There is nothing in *civic violence* or in the *violence of white supremacy* that adds up to world leadership. Indeed, these two facets of our society add up to abysmal moral failure.

The vision of Isaiah and Micah persists. It continues to provide for the nations of the world—and the United States!—a path to the alternative work of peacemaking. To that end, Micah adds a verse 5, one of the most remarkable verses in all of Scripture:

> For all the peoples walk,
> each in the name of its god,
> but we will walk in the name of the Lord our God
> forever and ever. (4:5)

In this curious verse we still have the vision of nations in procession. We still have the role of Israel to walk "in the name of YHWH our God." But remarkably, room is made in the procession for the presence of the other nations to walk, "each in the name of its god." The poet makes room for the presence, leadership, and legitimacy of other gods. He imagines that the other gods are also committed to a peace process. Thus Israel's walk in the procession did not require other nations to sign on to the God of Israel. Thus Micah compromises nothing of the specificity of Israel's faith. But that faith is not aggressive or exclusionary or preemptive but generous in its welcome. In such an enterprise, there is room for moral leadership, even for a moral center. That moral center, however, is not marked by swords and spears through which nations often prefer to posture. It is, rather, marked by plowshares and pruning hooks, by attending to the realities of life such as the provision for shared food. Much of that from the old prophet has been forgotten, as it was forgotten in ancient Israel. Happily, Merkel remembered her rootage in Luther even amid her dread days of East Germany. She put that memory to good use in her wise, courageous governance in a way that served the nations so well.

23

SLEEPLESS IN BABYLON

ALL AROUND US we are watching the "hewing down" of statues of erstwhile heroes of our nation, notably Robert E. Lee and Thomas Jefferson, and many others who have been deeply implicated in the long-running shame and disgrace of slavery. But what has especially drawn my attention to this subject is a chapter by Michel-Rolph Trouillot in his book, *Silencing the Past: Power and the Production of History* (1995/2015). Trouillot is a Haitian scholar who writes on the Haitian Revolution, the most dramatic and effective revolution in our hemisphere that ended French rule on the island. Trouillot completes his study with a review of the way in which Christopher Columbus was "produced" by the powerful to be made an untarnished icon, and then subsequently turned into an "American" whose "Day" we continue to celebrate. Trouillot shows how we have come full circle concerning Columbus so that now we are witness to a sustained effort to remove his statues from places of public prominence. Well behind Lee and Jefferson, Columbus represents the imposition of white European power on First Nation Americans. Given that cultural reality, his positive "image" can no longer be sustained among us.

The dismantling of statues of erstwhile heroes has led me, inescapably, to the nightmare of Nebuchadnezzar in Daniel 2. That powerful sixth-century Babylonian ruler, much despised by Israel had, it is reported to us, many sleepless nights, as he was "troubled" (Daniel 2:1, 3). In response to his nightmare, Nebuchadnezzar toys with his advisors. He insists they not only interpret his nightmare for him but also tell him the substance of his dream (vv. 3–11). But of course they cannot do it. They simply assert to the troubled king:

> *There is no one on earth who can reveal what the king*
> *demands! In fact no king, however great and powerful, has*
> *ever asked such a thing of any magician or enchanter or*
> *Chaldean. The thing that the king is asking is too difficult*
> *and no one can reveal it to the king except the gods, whose*
> *dwelling is not with mortals.* (v. 11)

Because they cannot decode the imperial nightmare, the lives of
the wise men are in jeopardy:

> *Because of this the king flew into a violent rage and*
> *commanded that all the wise men of Babylon be destroyed.*
> *The decree was issued, and the wise men were about to be*
> *executed; and they looked to Daniel and his companions to*
> *execute them.* (vv. 12–13)

But of course it is the Jewish exile, Daniel, to their rescue! Unlike
the king who is "troubled," and unlike the royal advisors who are
under great threat, Daniel is calm, cool, and calculating ("prudent and
discreet") and has no fear before the raging tyrant. There is a pause in
the narrative, while Daniel establishes and practices his Jewish creden-
tials as a sum of piety and faith (vv. 17–23). First, Daniel seeks "mercy
from the God of heaven" (v. 18). His bid for mercy shows that he is
a man of piety and faith, unlike Nebuchadnezzar, penultimate in his
capacity, and that he is on the receiving end of the juices of a good life.
His bid for mercy contrasts him with the Babylonian king who neither
asks for nor gives mercy. While the narrative does not comment on
his bid for mercy, it is obviously granted to him, as "the mystery was
revealed" (v. 19). What has been withheld from the imperial experts is
granted to the Jewish exile, a scenario that reiterates the wonder of the
narrative of Joseph before Pharaoh (Genesis 41:12–45). To complete
this pause for piety, Daniel breaks out in a blessing, rendering thanks
and praise to "the God of my ancestors" (vv. 20–23). Given this pause

for piety, Daniel is now fully ready and equipped to engage the troubled, sleepless, terrorizing king.

Daniel responds to the king by pointing out the deep contrast between the befuddled imperial experts and his own status before the God of heaven (vv. 27–30). What follows sounds like the bewildering complexity of a nightmare in which much is possible that would not occur in an awakened world of political realism. But of course that is why interpretation is required. First, Daniel must report on the substance of the nightmare (which the royal advisors could not do). The great statue of royal power moves from the precious beauty of gold to the fragile feet of clay, all of which is "broken in pieces." The statue is broken, moreover, by the "stone" and blown away by the "wind." So passes the proud governance of the statue of beauty and splendor!

Daniel's interpretation presents a sequence of kings that pass, one after another (vv. 36–45). The sequence begins in the *fine gold* of Babylon. Each successive regime is inferior to the preceding one, a second of *silver*, then a third of *bronze* and, finally, a fourth one of *iron* (vv. 37–40). But the feet of the fourth statue is only partly iron, but also partly clay:

> *As the toes of the feet were part iron and part clay, so the kingdom shall be partly strong and partly brittle. As you saw the iron mixed with clay, so will they mix with one another in marriage, but they will not hold together, just as iron does not mix with clay.* (vv. 42–43)

But then there is a counteraffirmation of another governance to the king:

> *And in the days of those kings the God of heaven will set up a kingdom that shall never be destroyed, nor shall this kingdom be left to another people. It shall crush all these kingdoms and bring them to an end, and it shall stand forever; just as you*

> *saw that a stone was cut from the mountain not by hands,*
> *and that it crushed the iron, the bronze, the clay, the silver,*
> *and the gold.* (vv. 44–45)

Daniel's interpretation moves from the description of the statue to the anticipation of the rise and fall of kingdoms and powers. Nowhere does Daniel speculate or become specific about the identity of the several kingdoms. That lack of identity has allowed great room for interpretation and identification of the several kings. It is plausible that the fourth king's regime of iron and clay is that of Antiochus IV from the time of the writing of the book of Daniel. But a focus too specific about the identity is sure to miss the point of the nightmare. The culmination of the dream is that the Kingdom of the God of heaven will ultimately prevail; all other pretenders will soon pass away and be forgotten. In the end none of the pretenders can stand before the force and will of the God of heaven who will prevail amid the historical-political process. Kingdoms come and go; they rise and fall. In a modern secular mode, Paul Kennedy, in *The Rise and Fall of the Great Powers: Economic Change and Military Conflict from 1500 to 2000* (1987), has traced the rise and fall of modern empires—Spanish, Dutch, English. His general thesis is that states "fall" when they have invested excessive amounts of money on the military that caused an economic imbalance. It requires little imagination to see that Kennedy's "causation" is readily recast in terms of the hubris of self-sufficiency, a hubris often performed by the old empires in the time of ancient Daniel. In either terms, modern-secular, or theological, empires rise and fall, prosper and then are forgotten:

> *Our little systems have their day;*
> *They have their day and cease to be;*
> *They are but broken lights of thee,*
> *And thou, O Lord, art more than they.*
> ("In Memoriam," Alfred Lord Tennyson [1850])

They cease to be! The would-be expansive rulers, in their hubris, are regularly shown to have "clay feet." With their clay feet at their base, the exhibit of much splendid gold at the top of their heads is unsustainable. Thus Daniel, in his rootage in God's "mercy," was able to observe the short shelf-life of every pretender who would fall in the face of the uncompromising rule of the God of heaven.

In the United States we are familiar enough with "clay feet" that we often choose not to notice that our vaunted "exceptionalism" is a quite short-run option. "Clay feet" turns out to be a major factor for even our most effective leaders:

- Thus Thomas Jefferson, for all of his eloquent wisdom, was an exploitative slave owner.
- Thus Abraham Lincoln, our wisest president, in his drive to secure "free soil" for yeomen like his father ruthlessly usurped Indian lands under treaty for the sake of white settlers.
- Thus Franklin Roosevelt, for all of his visionary passion, being blackmailed by a Southern Congress, permitted his great social legislation to be systemically racist so that government generosity was legally withheld from an important segment of the population.
- Thus Lyndon Johnson, he of great social progress on civil rights, was deeply diminished by his willing but foolish investment in Vietnam, an investment that overshadowed his superb achievements.
- Thus Ronald Reagan, a most popular conservative, was deeply implicated in the Iran–Contra deal, a secret arrangement that cynically outflanked the legal permit of the president.

We do not know whether these several presidents slept well at night. We may imagine that they were "troubled" enough that "sleep left them." We do know, from the many vexed photos of Lyndon Johnson in his "trouble," that he was markedly disturbed and could not cope easily with the problem of Vietnam he inherited or with the problem he made there for himself. It is impossible to imagine that Johnson did not have sleepless nights in DC, even as we know that Richard Nixon before him stalked the White House in the night, surely "sleepless in DC."

And now we have daily before us Vladimir Putin. We of course know nothing of his nights. But we can see, in broad daylight, the daring measure of his hubris. While Putin may in the end persist and prevail in Ukraine, we can see his clay feet in his gross miscalculation in that country. We are free to imagine that he is "sleepless in Moscow." Putin appears to proceed in his war as though he himself were ultimate and responsible to no one. Thus we may imagine, from our narrative text, that Putin, like so many others before him, has a *head of gold* in his bold violence, but stands on *feet of clay.*

The narrative of Daniel 2 has notably good outcomes. After the nightmare of Nebuchadnezzar and its interpretation two things happen. First, Nebuchadnezzar acknowledges his own penultimacy by presenting a grain offering to the God of heaven and by voicing a doxology to the God embraced by Daniel:

> *Truly, your God is God of gods and Lord of kings and a*
> *revealer of mysteries, for you have been able to reveal this*
> *mystery!* (v. 47)

Nebuchadnezzar made the same response in Daniel 4 when his sanity is restored to him:

> *I blessed the Most High,*
> *and praised and honored the one who lives forever.*
> *For his sovereignty is an everlasting sovereignty,*
> *and his kingdom endures from generation to generation.*
> *All the inhabitants of the earth are accounted as nothing,*
> *and he does what he wills with the host of heaven*

and the inhabitants of the earth.
There is no one who can stay his hand
or say to him, "What are you doing?" (4:34–35)

Now I, Nebuchadnezzar, praise and extol and honor the King
    of heaven,
for all his works are truth,
and his ways are justice;
and he is able to bring low those who walk in pride. (4:37)

We may judge that his "return of reason" was his recognition of his own penultimacy. That is, sanity is to acknowledge one's need to respond appropriately to the demands of holiness.

The second thing Nebuchadnezzar does in our chapter 2 is to promote Daniel, the exiled Jew, to be governor and leader of the wise who are skilled in statecraft. Thus, while we mark the "conversion" of Nebuchadnezzar into sane responsibility, we should not fail to notice and appreciate the courageous and transformative work of Daniel. Daniel sought no place in the empire. He relied on the gift given him in his piety and his faith. In the end the proud empire of Babylon came to rely upon this exiled Jew for the wise practice of statecraft. Daniel conceded nothing to Nebuchadnezzar and remained knowingly and confidently embedded in his tradition and in his faith.

While we may ponder "sleepless in Moscow" and in every other venue of power, we may also consider the practical wisdom entrusted to the faith community. It is wisdom marked by mercy! Conversely, not all the power, or might, or technical wisdom Nebuchadnezzar can muster is adequate for historical reality. The only reliable way through the life of the world is by way of mercy. Thus not only in Daniel 2:17 but also in 4:27, Daniel commends the gold-headed monarch to the God of mercy:

Therefore O king, may my counsel be acceptable to you:
atone for your sins with righteousness, and your iniquities

> *with mercy for the oppressed, so that your prosperity may be prolonged.* (4:27)

It turns out that mercy is the *sine qua non* for wellbeing in the world. Those who continue sleepless at night always keep relearning that truth, but always too late. By contrast there never was a time when Daniel and his ilk did not know that truth. Later, after Daniel, in his wisdom Jesus catalogued "the weightier matters of the Torah." Among the big three is "mercy":

> *You have neglected the weightier matters of the Torah: justice, mercy, faith!* (Matthew 23:23)

Such neglect causes sleeplessness; every time!

⚜ 24 ⚜

THE HOLY FOG OF WAR

No wisdom, no understanding, no counsel,
can avail against the Lord.
The horse is made ready for the day of battle,
but the victory belongs to the Lord. (Proverbs 21:30–31)

I WRITE THESE lines on the fifth day of the Russian invasion into
Ukraine. Thus far the war has been filled with surprise and unpredictability. Thus far Ukrainian resistance has been tougher, stiffer, and
more resilient than expected. Thus far the Russian military (with its
fragile supply lines) has been less effective than expected. Thus far
world opinion in rejecting the invasion (including protests in Russia,
restraint in China, and ambiguity in fascist Hungary) has been more
nearly unanimous and vigorous than had been expected. Of course no
one knows the outcome of the war, and events will surely evolve before
these lines of mine can be circulated.

Nonetheless the present circumstance of *tough resistance, military*
ineffectiveness, and *unanimous dissent* taken all together is enough to
pay attention to the lines of the Proverb quoted above. We may take
it that verse 30 lays down a deep conviction of the wisdom teachers in
ancient Israel, namely, that there is a hidden sovereignty of God present
and operative in the world that will not and cannot be penetrated
by human intelligence. This does not mean that there should not be
wisdom, smart calculation, and serious planning. It does mean, nonetheless, that such wisdom, smart planning, and serious preparation
should know, from the outset, that this work has a quite penultimate
quality to it. Of this deep caveat, Gerhard von Rad writes:

> *Its aim, rather, is to put a stop to the erroneous concept that*
> *a guarantee of success was to be found simply in practicing*
> *human wisdom and in making preparations. Man must*
> *always keep himself open to the activity of God, an activity*
> *which completely escapes all calculation, for between the*
> *putting into practice of the most reliable wisdom and that*
> *which then actually takes place, there always lies a great*
> *unknown.* (*Wisdom in Israel* [1972], 101)

Thus the saying bears witness to the "wild card" in human affairs that is beyond human control. Beyond that, moreover, the saying dares to link that *wild card* to *the holiness of God* that is pervaded, in varying ways, with divine righteousness, justice, compassion, faithfulness, and truthfulness. The saying is characteristically elusive so that God's working will not be pinned down in any precise way. The saying is a recognition that qualifies human wisdom, understanding, and counsel in retrospect. In the wake of these five long days in Ukraine, we already have sufficient data to see that the best wisdom and understanding could not have anticipated the tentative outcomes of *toughness, ineffectiveness*, and *unanimity*. The formula of the proverb refuses precision exactly because it concerns the holiness of God who operates in hiddenness and in freedom. And, of course, this elusive reference to God allows that some unexpected "slippage" can be explained and justified in other ways, if we choose to do so.

Verse 30 nonetheless invites us to reflect on the God to whom the Proverb bears witness. It is to be noticed that no active verbs are assigned to God; we plausibly do not have to do here with the emancipatory God of the Exodus or the covenant-enforcing God of the prophets. Rather, we have here the remote inscrutable God of the sapiential tradition who works in ways we cannot identify or measure. Which is why we sing:

> *God is working his purpose out as year succeeds to year;*
> *God is working his purpose out, and the time is drawing near;*

Nearer and nearer draws the time, the time that shall surely be,
When the earth shall be filled with the glory of God
As the waters cover the sea.

("God Is Working His Purpose Out,"
Arthur Campbell Ainger [1894])

God moves in a mysterious way His wonders to perform;
He plants his footsteps in the sea and rides upon the storm.
Deep in unfathomable mines of never failing skill
He treasures up his bright designs and works His sov'reign will.
His purposes will ripen fast unfolding every hour;
The bud may have a bitter taste but sweet will be the flow'r.
Blind unbelief is sure to err and scan His work in vain;
God is His own interpreter, and he will make it plain.

("God Moves in a Mysterious Way,"
William Cowper [1774])

This is the God attested in the prophetic formulation of Isaiah 14:24, 26–27:

The Lord of hosts has sworn:
As I have designed, so shall it be;
and as I have planned, so shall it come to pass . . .
This is the plan that is planned concerning the whole earth;
and this is the hand that is stretched out over all the nations.
For the Lord of hosts has planned and who will annul it?
His hand is stretched out, and who will turn it back?

To be sure, this prophetic declaration is filled out with an active verb in verse 25, but the primary accent in this prophetic utterance is less clear about implementation. Thus God's work is hidden and functions in this text primarily to curb unacceptable human conduct:

> *Hardly anything was said about "cooperation" or*
> *"accompaniment" on the part of Yahweh. One knew about*
> *him, but in this business of discovering an order, Yahweh*
> *only appeared, on the whole, more in the sense of a limitation*
> *imposed on men.* (Von Rad, *Wisdom in Israel,* 399–400)

Thus limit is imposed on human wisdom, understanding, and counsel. Limit is placed on military plans and on political resolve. And no matter how much technology, manpower, or equipment can be mustered, human reason cannot and will not transgress that limit.

At the moment the invasion of Russia into Ukraine is a replication of the long-running military action of the United States in Vietnam. All the money, all the technology, all the equipment, and all the manpower gave the United States an illusionary edge in the war with the Viet Cong, an edge that left US presidents and military planners confident in their work. But of course all of that "successful" preparation cut no ice in the reality of combat. In his retrospect after the war and an acknowledgment of his shameless leadership, Robert McNamara, secretary of defense, utilized the telling phrase, "the fog of war" (James G. Blight and Janet M. Lang, *The Fog of War: Eleven Lessons Learned from the Life of Robert S. McNamara* [2005]). As soon as combat begins, there is fog of bewilderment and confusion that quickly overrides careful planning. (There are important exceptions to that, as is the case of the German planners who, in World War I, calculated the exact movement of troops by train into France.) Speaking of that same war, McGeorge Bundy, a guiding leader of the war who sneered at its protesters, said in a final retrospect, "We were very smart, but we were not as smart as we thought we were." (I can no longer identify the quote that I read a long time ago.) So it is, over and over, that the fog of war teaches us that we were not as smart as we thought we were!

To McNamara's phrase I have added only "Holy." It is enough talk of the fog of war that at the moment overwhelms the careful

Russian calculation. If, however, we follow our proverb, it is not mere "fog." It is fog dispatched by the Holy One of Israel; presumably this mighty God can dispatch fog in the same way that frogs, hail, and gnats were dispatched in the plagues of Egypt (see Exodus 7–10).

Verse 31 takes the general principle enunciated in verse 30 and applies it to military planning. The saying acknowledges the best military equipment on offer, "horses." The military planners are always relying on "horses" (i.e., on tanks, bombs, and missiles). Thus the representative of Assyria in ancient Jerusalem is so sure of Assyrian horses that he is willing to toy with the feeble Israelites:

> *Come now, make a wager with my master the king of Assyria. I will give you two thousand horses, if you are able on your part to set riders on them. How can you repulse a single captain among the least of my master's servants, when you rely on Egypt for chariots and for horsemen?* (Isaiah 36:8–9)

Even the Assyrian, however, mediated through Israelite dialect, can recognize that horses are penultimate:

> *Moreover, is it without the Lord that I have come up against this land to destroy it?*
> *The Lord said to me, Go up against this land and destroy it.*
> (v. 10)

Thus he claims to be fighting the battle of YHWH, as the God of Israel has turned against Israel. Indeed, Isaiah can warn his people that reliance on horses is a futile enterprise:

> *Alas for those who go down to Egypt for help*
> *and who rely in horses,*
> *who trust in chariots because they are many*

and in horsemen because they are very strong,
but do not look to the Holy One of Israel or consult the Lord!
    (Isaiah 31:1)

It is the same with military planners:

Oh, rebellious children, says the Lord,
who carry out a plan, but not mine;
who make an alliance, but against my will,
adding sin to sin;
who set out to go down to Egypt without asking for my counsel,
to take refuge in the protection of Pharaoh,
and to seek shelter in the shadow of Egypt. (Isaiah 30:1–2)

Horses can be made ready! But victory (*teshua*) belongs not to the horses, nor to the horsemen, nor to the military planners. It belongs to God! Still no active verb! YHWH doesn't "do" anything! It is as though YHWH simply waits for events to turn as willed: keeping watch over God's own! Wait as limit; wait as holy purpose; wait as the creator, perhaps wait in solidarity with "the least." More one cannot say. And more the proverb does not claim. It is enough. Do not imagine the cunning of human history without the overriding of holiness. Do not be so impressed with technological capacity as to think it is the clue to wellbeing. Do not give in to the pride that our ways are adequate or will prevail because they will not (see Isaiah 55:8–9).

Religious communities—and thus the church—are the only venues in town in which this *unmanaged holiness* can be talked about. The Holy One who may dispatch fog is no chaplain of a nation, is not a patron of one's side in war, and is not a nice uncle who offers consolation. This rather is a God who will not be mocked, not by all the hubris we may muster. Thus the king in ancient Jerusalem can hope:

> *It may be that the Lord our God has heard the words of the*
> *Rabshakeh, whom his master the king of Assyria has sent to*
> *mock the living God, and will rebuke the words that the Lord*
> *our God has heard.* (Isaiah 37:4)

Thus the king prays:

> *O Lord of hosts, God of Israel, who are enthroned above the*
> *cherubim, you are God, you alone, of all the kingdoms of the*
> *earth; you have made heaven and earth. Incline your ear, O*
> *Lord, and hear; open your eyes, O Lord, and see; hear all the*
> *words of Sennacherib, which he has sent to mock the living*
> *God. . . . So now, O Lord our God, save us from his hand, so*
> *that all the kingdoms of the earth may know that you alone*
> *are the Lord.* (Isaiah 37:16–20)

There is doxology addressed to YHWH; there is a description of the threat in case God has not noticed; and there is petition: "Save us." The prophetic response to the prayer of the king picks up on the theme of "mocking":

> *Whom have you mocked and reviled?*
> *Against whom have you raised your voice*
>   *and haughtily lifted your eyes?*
> *Against the Holy One of Israel!*
> *By your servants you have mocked the Lord,*
>   *and you have said,*
> *"With my many chariots I have gone up to*
>   *the heights of the mountains,*
>   *to the far recesses of Lebanon;*
> *I felled its tallest cedars, its choicest cypresses;*
> *I came to its remotest height, its densest forest.*
> *I dug wells and drank waters,*

> *I dried up with the sole of my foot*
> > *all the streams of Egypt."* (37:23–25)

The Assyrian overlord is filled with the "I" of royal arrogance. But then the divine resolve:

> *Because you have raged against me*
> *and your arrogance has come to my ears,*
> *I will put my hook in your nose*
> *and my bit in your mouth;*
> *I will turn you back on the way by which you came.*
> (Isaiah 37:29)

God in God's holiness will not be mocked, not by the violence of war, not by the arrogance of invasion, not by the merciless indifference of the strong against the weak, not by the planning that is scientifically perfect and technologically effective, not by all the hubris we can muster.

And we in the church get to talk about this! We are summoned out of our complacent church theology, out of our comfortable context of vexed families, and out of our easy talk of love and forgiveness. We are summoned to the daring claim of divine sovereignty in a world seemingly ordered according to the will of the ones with the most horses. The horses may have their way in war. The counsel of wisdom and understanding might provisionally prevail. But we are left to speak about the One who is not greatly impressed with horses, but has another purpose for the world. The odd claim entrusted to us is that this purpose is now at work in, with, and under the ordeals of the day. This holy purpose will not be identified with the United States or with Russia. It is this *holy fog* that gives cover to the vulnerable, that gives vexation to the proud, and that precludes excessive human management. The one of whom we speak is, in a moment of inexplicable emancipation, dubbed as a warrior, even as "a man of war."

The Lord is a warrior; the Lord is his name.
Pharaoh's chariots and his army he cast into the sea;
his picked officers were sunk in the Red Sea.
The floods covered them; they went down into the depths like a
stone.
Your right hand, O Lord, glorious in power—
your right hand, O Lord, shattered the enemy....
The Lord will reign forever and ever. (Exodus 15:3–6, 18)

Part V

REFLECTIONS MORE PERSONAL

❧ 25 ❧

DIVINE ARITHMETIC!

NOW THAT I have just turned eighty-nine, it is inescapable that I think, from time to time, of my ending. Sometimes I think of my longevity and am amazed. Sometimes—not often—I think of my death. I am mostly content to leave that in God's good hands. I am aware that this thinking might well change for me if I face a long disability or some form of long-term suffering. Mostly I think of "fullness of days," a phrase used to characterize Job's ending (Job 42:17). This phrase does not specify age or longevity but refers to the quality or content of one's life. "Fullness of days" might be used, variously, to refer to the completion of one's bucket list, or a sense of having been useful and made a difference, or having lived in sync with one's creator. None of that is specified for Job. And I specify none of it yet for me, except to notice that in my "fullness of days" I have been remarkably blessed, and I have so much for which to give great thanks.

My thought about "fullness of days" is enough for you to see why I was drawn to this report on Queen Elizabeth I. In her old age, reports Edith Weir Perry in *Under the Tudors: Being the Story of Matthew Parker Sometime Archbishop of Canterbury* (1964, 256), the Bishop of St. Davids preached to the queen on the text, "Lord, teach us to number our days, that we may apply our hearts to wisdom." The Queen cried out angrily, that

"He might have kept his arithmetic to himself."

Perry does not specify the pronouns in the queen's statement, "he, himself," whether the queen intended that the Bishop of St. Davids should keep his arithmetic to himself, or whether God, in the psalm quoted, has God's own arithmetic. I choose to think it is the latter, thus a reference to "divine arithmetic." If we take that reading of it, then the queen did not want to know of the ways in which God reckons human longevity, and certainly not the way God may have reckoned the lifespan of the aging queen, a lady who was quite accustomed to having her own say and her own way. Either way, the statement of the queen set me to thinking about my own "fullness of days," and the "divine arithmetic" that pertains to my life.

The psalm that the Bishop of St. Davids quotes is Psalm 90, surely a poem/prayer preoccupied with God's arithmetic. The psalm voices the mighty contrast between *the reality of God* who is "from everlasting to everlasting" (v. 2) and *human life* that is brief and faces limits set by the ordering of the creator God. (Of course one can say that human life is "short" without following Thomas Hobbes to say "nasty, brutish, short.") The psalm concerns how the brevity of our human life is to be computed in the context of divine durability. In verse 10 the psalm recognizes the inescapable durability and limit of human possibility:

> *The days of our life are seventy years,*
> *or perhaps eighty, if we are strong.* (v. 10)

Of course these numbers can be amended according to our scientific advances that may extend human longevity, but such human gains do not change the elemental difference between *God's eternity* and *human transience.* The verse recognizes, moreover, that however human life may indeed be extended, it is a venue for restlessness and trouble that are intrinsically "the human predicament":

> *Even then their span is only toil and trouble;*
> *they are soon gone, and we fly away.* (v. 10)

The psalm acknowledges that human longevity has uncrossable limitation, and any pretense of durable autonomy is an alienating illusion.

Verse 12 advances from verse 10 to recognize that an honest aware-ness of that uncrossable limitation is an act of wisdom. Conversely, a refusal to recognize that reality of limit is an act of supreme foolishness. Once there is wisdom enough to recognize and accept that reality, the psalmist can move on in verses 13–14 to count on God's compassion and steadfast love that may bring gladness. The psalm pivots on the double "turn." In verse 3, human persons are summoned to *"turn" back from autonomy* to accept in verse 4 the ultimacy of God's reckoning of time. In verse 13 the psalmist bids God to *"turn" towards compassion.* Thus the psalm antic-ipates a recalibration of full covenantal interaction in which the reality and gift of divine governance are operative and embraced, and in which the realities of human limit and contingency are honestly faced. Thus the psalmist, in the end, gladly submits to divine arithmetic. On that basis the psalmist can hope for and trust in the "prospering" of human achievement (v. 17). The psalm itself invites us into the process of recalibrating our lives according to the nonnegotiable reality of divine governance and human transience. Once that reality is embraced, there is ample reason for trust and gladness. Or in our phrasing, one may accept one's "fullness of days."

In light of this process, I thought some more about "divine arith-metic" that so irritated the queen. I could think of three instances in Scripture of "divine arithmetic" that confounds our otherwise normal calculation. The reader may think of other instances as well.

In the book of Judges, Israel was mightily beset by the Midianites, so much so that Gideon (Jerubbaal) recruited a mighty army to oppose the Midianites. Before the battle can be mounted, however, YHWH objects to the size of Gideon's army and requires that Gideon send many of his troops home. YHWH explains the requirement to Gideon:

> *The troops with you are too many for me to give the*
> *Midianites into their hand. Israel would only take the credit*
> *away from me, saying, "My own hand has delivered me."*

The narrative reports that Gideon sent 22,000 soldiers home and kept 10,000 fighting men. But again YHWH objects:

> *The troops are still too many; take them down to the water*
> *and I will sift them out for you there.* (v. 4)

YHWH's method of "sifting out" soldiers to retain is to test them by having them drink water from a pool. The majority lapped water out of the pool like a dog, with their heads down so that they are exposed and vulnerable, and so are rejected. The ones who drank water from their hands and kept their heads up in vigilance were the ones retained for the battle. The three hundred who were retained were sufficient to win a mighty victory for Israel. YHWH had calculated that three hundred soldiers were enough for the battle when they were the right three hundred. There was no need for a bigger number, even though conventional military wisdom may have thought they were needed. YHWH knew otherwise and better, and so confounded conventional military wisdom (see Proverbs 21:30–31).

In II Kings 6:8–23 Israel, as usual, was at war with Syria. The unnamed king of Syria had become convinced that Elisha was a spy for Israel who must be eliminated. To that end he surrounded Elisha's house with "an army with horses and chariots," a mighty force. Elisha's aide observes that threatening force and is appropriately frightened. By contrast Elisha remains calm and unconcerned. He comforts his aide by saying,

> *Do not be afraid, for there are more with us than there are*
> *with them.* (v. 16)

The aide of course can see and can count. He sees that there are exactly two of them (he and his master), opposed by a great enemy force. For an instant he imagines that Elisha has miscounted. But then Elisha prays that his aide may have other eyes to see more clearly, and he saw!

> *The mountain was full of horses and chariots of fire all*
> *around Elisha.* (v. 17)

It turned out that Elisha knew and saw what his aide had not seen; he had counted correctly! The horses and chariots of fire dispatched by YHWH were more than that of the Syrian forces. As a consequence, the Syrians were struck blind, easily defeated, and led into the city where Elisha commanded the unnamed Israelite king to host a great feast for the erstwhile enemy. For a time, in the wake of the feast, the war subsided. Everything, it turns out, depended on divine arithmetic. Everything depended on the resources of YHWH being larger than those of the Syrians. So it was, even though neither the Syrians nor the aide of Elisha could, on their own, see the reality of this alternative arithmetic.

In the parable of Jesus in Matthew 20:1–16, the ordinary assumptions of labor and capital are upended. The parable teems with numbers:

Nine o'clock. (v. 3)
Three o'clock. (v. 5)
Five o'clock. (v. 6)
One hour. (v. 12)

The point is unmistakable. The vineyard workers were not paid according to the amount of work they did. They were all paid the same because of the inexplicable generosity of the owner who counted working hours differently. It is no wonder that the ones who worked the longest grumbled:

> *These last worked only one hour, and you have made them equal to us who have borne the burden of the day and the scorching heat.* (v. 12)

The workers had arithmetic on their side: so much work . . . so much pay! They were grounded in a commonsense appeal to normal arithmetic that was beyond dispute. The countertheme of the owner, to the contrary, is introduced inside the parable in verse 8, where the workers who came *last* are paid *first*. In the reflective commentary of Jesus in verse 16 the point is reiterated, now beyond the parable to the larger reality of divine arithmetic:

So the last will be first, and the first will be last. (v. 16)

John Donahue can write of this parable:

> *Hardly any parable in the Gospels seems to upset the basic structure of an orderly society as does this one. . . . Though Matthew is in debt to his Jewish heritage in his understanding of justice, he redefines justice in terms of God's generous and saving intervention on behalf of those whom others might see as outside the pale of God's care. God's justice is different from human justice. It forgives unpayable debts and summons disciples to live a life of forgiveness to others as an expression of gratitude.* (John Donahue, *The Gospel in Parables* [1988], 81, 84)

Donahue concludes:

> *God's ways are not human ways. Those categories of worth and value which people erect to separate themselves from others are reversed in God's eyes. If divine freedom is limited by human conceptions of God's goodness, men and women may never be able to experience unmerited goodness.* (85)

When we consider these three instances of divine arithmetic, the common claim of the three is breathtaking. It turns out that the ordinary calculation of the world is overturned:

- Gideon needed only a small number of soldiers who are allied with the force of God.
- Elisha and his aide are kept safe by horses and chariots of fire about which the Syrians did not know and which they could not see.

- The Lord of the vineyard pays in generosity well beyond any conventional *quid pro quo.*

In every case, the divine arithmetic outruns human calculation. The old Queen Elizabeth did not want to know about the divine arithmetic of "three score and ten, or four score." She did not want to count her days because she could recognize that there were only a few left to her. But divine arithmetic does its calculation in spite of us. It does not count by our preferred numbers. It relies on "fullness of days," however, many there may be. Our most familiar rendition of divine arithmetic, I suppose, is the great hymn of Isaac Watts:

> *A thousand ages in thy sight are like an evening gone,*
> *short as the watch that ends the night before the rising sun.*
> *Time, like an ever rolling stream, bears all our years away;*
> *they fly forgotten, as a dream dies at the opening day.*
> ("Our God, Our Help in Ages Past,"
> in *Glory to God* [2013], 687)

Notice the strange arithmetic:

A thousand ages = an evening gone!

The hymn concerns the eternal abiding of the Holy One of Israel, contra the feeble, fearful calculus of human longevity. The hymn itself is an exercise of yielding our transience to the reliability of God's abiding faithfulness that keeps us safe beyond all times.

No doubt we will continue to utilize our human arithmetic whereby we do our best measurements:

- We will measure our productivity in whatever line of work we have . . . the number of pastoral calls, the number of published articles, or whatever.

- We will continue to measure our intelligence by various IQ tests of all kinds, even continuing after we notice how biased they surely are.
- We will continue to measure our enormous wealth, whereby the billionaires strut and posture among us, listing the four hundred richest women in the world, etc.
- We will continue to value excessively the measure of our Gross National Product.
- We will continue to measure our military capacity, comparing our arsenal of bombs and tanks to that of our adversaries.
- We will continue to urge our children to excel at the best grades, or the best performance, or the best shot put.

But then, in an instant of sober honesty and realism, we may come to see, from time to time, how flimsy and unimportant are our measurements. We may notice that our arithmetic amounts to very little of significance in the face of our long-term life with God. Such sober reality tends to come upon us in our moments of vulnerability and helplessness when we notice that our "big numbers" of productivity, wealth, intelligence, or power are of no use to us. We might even withdraw from the rat race of measurement for an alternative life. When we withdraw from the rat race we may stop our intense passion for our big numbers. This is exactly the invitation of Jeremiah, who invites us away from the measurable categories of wisdom, might, and wealth:

> *Do not let the wise boast in their wisdom, do not let the*
> *mighty boast in their might, do not let the wealthy boast in*
> *their wealth; but let those who boast boast in this, that they*
> *understand and know me, that I am the Lord; I act with*
> *steadfast love, justice and righteousness in the earth, for in*
> *these things I delight, says the Lord.* (Jeremiah 9:23–24)

We can measure our wisdom, might, and wealth. But when we stop these eager calculations, we may fall, as the prophet intends, into the practice of steadfast love, justice, and righteousness. But of course our usual arithmetic does not work in these categories. We have to take up a different set of calculations. This may be exactly what Jesus had in mind when he listed the elements for entry into a different future:

> *I was hungry and you gave me food, I was thirsty and you gave me something to drink, I was a stranger and you welcomed me, I was naked and you gave me clothing, I was sick and you took care of me, I was in prison and you visited me.* (Matthew 25:35–36)

Thus as I pursue my ninetieth year, on my best days I imagine that my longevity is of little import. Much more crucial is "fullness of days." The Torah, and Jesus after the Torah, has in mind exactly "full of days" of neighborly covenantalism. It turns out that the God who is "our hope for years to come" is not a scorekeeper, but a neighborhood administrator who is quite uninterested in our best measurements. Methinks the good queen did not get it. And most of us, most of the time, do not get it. But sometimes some of us do. And then there is rejoicing in "our eternal home."

26

DUGOUT DIALOGUES

WITH A LOAN from my friend, Allen Horstman, I have been reading a most remarkable book, *K: A History of Baseball in Ten Pitches* by Tyler Kepner (2019). Every baseball fan will know and take the cue that "K" is the proper entry on a scorecard for a strikeout. The book is organized in ten chapters, each one concerning a particular baseball pitch, for example, fast ball, curve, slider, knuckle ball, et cetera. Each chapter is a leisurely, gossipy discussion of a particular pitch, who threw it best, how each pitcher learned it, and what the pitch caused to happen to the pitcher who threw it.

What surprised me most about the book is the report of a congenial, convivial network of pitchers. Not only did they compete fiercely with each other, but they also observed each other, learned from each other, and taught each other, sharing their "secrets" of success. There is also generous instruction from senior and retired players and managerial types. It is a truism that every pitcher must have at least three effective pitches, two plus a good fastball. And if one of those pitches fails, then the pitcher must compensate and adjust, and experiment with a new pitch. The book in particular calls attention to three teachers who helped pitchers develop new pitches:

- Fred Martin, for a time a member of my beloved St. Louis Cardinals, in his retirement taught Bruce Sutter, Roger Craig, and Donnie Moore the art of the splitter. The chapter details the remarkable success of Sutter on his way to the Hall of Fame.
- Johnny Podres was a master of the change-up and taught it successfully to Curt Shilling, Bobby Ojeda, and Frank Viola.

- Perhaps most important is Johnny Sain, a serious student of the game. He taught the slider to John Smoltz, Tommy John, and a series of other players. There is even a photo of "the great Johnny Sain" teaching from the mound, surrounded by Tiger pitchers including Johnny Podres.

The book evidences *a network of practical mutual assistance, functioning to help different members of the network to better their skills and gain effectiveness in their work.* Thus I am able to imagine an ongoing conversation in the dugout before, during, and after the game, especially among pitchers on their off-days when they have time for such helpful talk.

Given that characterization of the conversation in the dugout, it occurred to me that it might be a useful formulation that accurately describes a well-functioning congregation: *A network of practical mutual assistance, functioning to help different members of the network to better their skills and gain effectiveness in their work.* By way of transfer from baseball to congregational life, I have often reiterated my conviction that the three most elemental practices of the Christian life are:

1. Generosity
2. Hospitality
3. Forgiveness

One could quibble with that list, but assume it for now. What if we think about these three "best pitches" of the Christian life, with a network helping us to improve our skills at these aspects of our "proper work"? This would suggest that the congregation is in the process of nurturing, sustaining, and encouraging such intentional growth. So consider:

1. *Generosity as the fast ball of faith.* It is a given in baseball that a good pitcher must have a good fast ball above all else. Everything else depends on a good fast ball. Thus I suggest that, for a

faithful Christian life, everything begins with and depends upon generosity, the capacity and willingness to share resources with the neighborhood in the hope of contributing to the wellbeing of the whole. Such generosity surely includes good "steward-ship" for the wellbeing of the congregation, but it also includes contributions to the body politic that takes the form of generous charity, and generous tax-supported policies that enhance the neighborhood and attend to those who lack adequate resources.

2. *Hospitality as the curve ball of faith.* A central feature of a good curve ball is that it surprises the batter. Such a pitch requires just the right twist, the snap of the wrist in order that the batter will be surprised; such a pitch depends to some great extent on deception. Hospitality in a society marked by anxiety and fear is always a surprise, given our systemic fear of the other. Church faith depends upon such hospitality, the welcome for the stranger, and openness to the other who is unlike us. As I write this, our newspaper is running reports (from the AP) about inhabitants in the Alps at the border of Italy and France who welcome Moroccan immigrants who risk their lives at the crossing. It is reported that in the Alps there is,

> *a network of hundreds of volunteers who run migrant shelters, clothe those in need for the hazardous crossing and trek in the cold . . . .Armed with thermoses of hot tea and the belief that their own humanity would be diminished if they left pregnant women, children and men young and old to fend for themselves, the Alpine helpers are a counter-argument to populist politicians.*
> ("Freezing in the Alps, Migrants Find Warm Hearts and Comfort," *Record-Eagle,* December 22, 2021, A6)

Such hospitality is always a surprise because it boldly contra-dicts our ready propensity to exclusion in fear. Faith acts out the counterargument!

3. *Forgiveness as the spitball of faith.* The spitball is outlawed in baseball. Nonetheless certain identifiable pitchers, notably Gaylord Perry, threw it and enjoyed the widespread impression that they were throwing it. I suggest that forgiveness is as illegitimate as a spitball in our society. Within predatory capitalism, forgiveness is indeed banned and illegal because forgiveness of a serious kind would disrupt and eventually dismantle an economy of predatory greed. Forgiveness breaks the destructive cycle of *quid pro quo* that always champions austerity toward the disadvantaged. As I write this Senator Joe Manchin has just announced his opposition to Biden's Build Back Better program because, says he, someone might spend the money foolishly. The senator makes the oldest, most jaded, cynical excuse for parsimony and a refusal to forgive such disadvantage. Manchin, moreover, can say this, while he lives in DC on a luxurious yacht and drives a Lamborghini. But in the *quid pro quo* world of the senator, worry that the disadvantaged might get an "unearned" gain sets off the alarms. Forgiveness of debts is so dangerous because it undermines the grip of fear and the leverage of guilt wherein some are kept perpetually in hock to others. But faith does not mind such "civil disobedience" in the service of "love of neighbor."

So imagine Christians in a congregation in an ongoing dugout conversation about these best pitches of faith, and how to improve our skill and capacity with them, how to be more effective in generosity, how to be bolder in hospitality, and how to be more subversive in forgiveness.

How to pitch generosity that need hold nothing back;
How to pitch hospitality that welcomes without fear,
How to pitch forgiveness that breaks the vicious cycles of
     retaliation.

This triad might be the basis for a curriculum in the congregation for the nurture of the young, for initiation of young adults who have never thought about such matters, and for other members who have long known this and forgotten. The substance for such a congregational curriculum might go like this. Simply identify the best witnesses for each of these pitches. Identify *the most generous members* of the network, not the ones who give the most, but the ones who give most readily and most freely. Identify the members of the network *who best practice welcome of strangers*, who may do so in unnoticed ways. Identify the members of the network who have been *most forgiven* and who have received new life from forgiveness. Good education is narrative work. Let the stories be told. Let the congregation be on the receiving end of such truth-telling. Let the congregation celebrate these narratives that defy the old rules of *parsimony, exclusion*, and *score-keeping*. The stories are contagious. Hearing such stories is sure to evoke other possibilities and permit risk-taking in fresh forms.

I had one other impression from Kepner's book. The pitchers and coaches of pitchers engage in long-term practice. It might indeed take a year to perfect a new pitch. The embrace of a life of generosity, hospitality, and forgiveness is a long-term project. One reason it is long-term work is that in our society we have so much to unlearn. The unlearning and the relearning is not a head trip. It is actual practice, the very doing of these actions and, consequently, the amazing capacity of watching the neighborhood being transformed before our very eyes. When a new pitch works, everyone notices; when a fast ball pops, or when a curve breaks, or when a spitball affronts, everyone in the dugout notices. Games turn out differently. And the cloud of witnesses in the stands joins in the elation.

God's baseball time: "A thousand ages in thy sight are like a season gone."

27

NORMAN GOTTWALD

NORMAN GOTTWALD HAS died at ninety-five. He is, in my judgment, the most important and influential Old Testament scholar of the twentieth century in the United States. (The only other near candidate for that, in my judgment, is Brevard Childs who died in 2007.) In 1979, Gottwald published his discipline-redefining opus, *The Tribes of Yahweh: A Sociology of the Religion of Liberated Israel, 1250–1050 bc* (see my early review of Gottwald's book in *The Journal of the American Academy of Religion* 48 [1980]: 441–51). Perhaps there is some irony in the fact that Childs also published his discipline-redefining work, *Introduction to the Old Testament as Scripture*, in the same year. Thus 1979 was a major pivot point in the discipline, as these two lead scholars moved, in very different ways, beyond conventional historical social criticism that had dominated study in the modern era. It was characteristic of Gottwald's generous, irenic way that he published an article showing how his work and the work of Childs could be constructively held together in a useful, critical way ("Social Matrix and Canonical Shape," *Theology Today* 42, no. 3 [1985]: 307–21).

Gottwald's book is of durable significance because, in a quite frontal way, he set out to read the Old Testament with reference to the interpretive categories of the social sciences, notably the function of economics. Specifically, he focused on the period of the book of Judges and the "tribal" configuration in Israel before the emergence of the monarchy. He reviewed and rejected the notion that there was a violent "conquest" of the land by the invasive, intrusive Israelites from Egypt. In like manner, he reviewed and rejected the German hypothesis that the land was settled by "immigrants." Positively, he championed the thesis that the conflict narrated in the book of Judges was the result of a "Peasant Revolt" whereby the subsistence agricultural peasants in Canaan violently revolted against the Canaanite city-kings and aggressive landowners who acted in predatory, exploitative ways toward the vulnerable peasants. That is, he proposed that the narrative reflects something of a class conflict.

In order to fund the imagination, courage, and energy of such a peasant movement, Gottwald proposed that the Pentateuchal traditions may be understood, in sum and substance, as the "ideology" that was celebrated and reiterated in cultic context. This regular public reiteration of the narratives provided coherence and justification for "the revolt." It was inescapable that along with such a hypothesis of a cultic recital of a justifying "ideology" would come the question of the role of YHWH, the God featured in the "ideological" narratives of the Pentateuch. Gottwald proceeded very carefully to distinguish his approach that he termed "Structural Functionalism" from the usual "religious idealism" that keeps YHWH as an independent agent quite distinct from social reality. Gottwald concludes that "mono-Yahwism" is a "function" of "sociopolitical equality."

> *The loosely federated egalitarian tribalism of Israel was symbolized and institutionalized at the most comprehensive level by a common cultic-ideological allegiance to mono-Yahwism. . . . Accordingly, my functional proposition that mono-Yahwism was dependably related to communal egalitarianism leads us to see that mono-Yahwism, far from being an eccentric, cultic compartment of Israel's life or an arbitrary ornament on the main body of society, was in fact of critical significance as the axial, form-giving, and energy-releasing reality in literary and intellectual culture, in economics, in social organization, in military affairs, and in self-government. (The Tribes of Yahweh, 615–16)*

It follows immediately for Gottwald that the reverse proposition is also the case: "Sociopolitical egalitarianism was a function of mono-Yahwism" (616). In these reciprocal formulations YHWH and social egalitarianism are intimately and exclusively held together. Thus belief in YHWH is accepted

> . . . *as the motivator and sanctioner of the social system, together with his cult's minimal demands on the resources and on political power,* [which] *met the two potentially contradictory communal needs for cultural identity and unified self-defense against rival systems, on the one hand, and for egalitarianism and self-rule, on the other hand.* (619–20)

Thus in the confessional life of early Israel YHWH is inescapably and integrally linked to a certain view of and certain practice of economic egalitarianism. It is impossible to overstate the importance of this daring claim by Gottwald that is at the heart of his study. This two-way articulation of "function" means that Israel cannot "have" YHWH without the social vision and social practice of neighborly covenantalism. Conversely, this means that in context Israel could not have such a social practice and vision except as it was linked to YHWH. It may be readily inferred from Gottwald that the counterpoint is also true. Canaan could not have its predatory city-king economic system without Ba'al, and Ba'al could not be embraced without the embrace of a predatory economy, for Ba'al is (in the horizon of Israel) the great lord and legitimator of economic predation. This linkage is evident if we consider, at the same time, *the dramatic "contest" at Mt. Carmel between YHWH and Ba'al* (I Kings 18), a contest of gods, and the *narrative of Naboth's vineyard, a dispute about land* (I Kings 21). Ahab and Jezebel, as followers of and advocates for Ba'al, felt legitimate in seizing peasant land, even as Elijah, an advocate for YHWH, speaks a harsh word on behalf of the peasant interest of Naboth. This linkage is defining for

Gottwald and is a central teaching that we may learn to take seriously as we observe the same linkage everywhere in both the Old and New Testaments. A key distortion of biblical faith, in Gottwald's frame of reference, is the widespread, endlessly recurring attempt to have the God of the Bible without the socioeconomic practice that goes with that God. When that linkage is not deliberately maintained, both the God of Israel (the God of the Gospel!) and the social economic practice of the community are sure to be distorted.

It is illuminating to take into account the immediate cultural context in which Gottwald did his remarkable work. In larger context, he worked in the midst of an emerging "liberation theology" that was much informed by Marxian categories of analysis. Much more specifically, Gottwald lived and worked in the Bay area as a faculty member of the Graduate Theological Union amid the wake of the Vietnam War and at the time of the "free speech movement" in the university that pitted protesting students against the quite unresponsive administration of the university that was backed and supported in its intransigence by the ideological fervor of Governor Reagan and his Board of Regents. It is easy enough to see that the conflict (conflict between the gods and conflict between social systems) that Gottwald discerned in the biblical tradition was being reperformed before his very eyes! Lest we judge that Gottwald's hypothesis of a "peasant revolt" was for him too personal and subjective, we may notice that it has been observed that the German hypothesis of "immigration" nicely echoes the Bismarckian formation of the German state, just as the American model of "conquest" reflects the European colonialization of the American continent. No interpretation is ever innocent about such matters, and Gottwald surely was not.

As is invariably the case with such a daring hypothesis, Gottwald's book has required many refinements over time, the correction of some overstatements, and the elimination of some materials that turned out to be elementally distractive. On the main point, however, Gottwald's scholarship has decisively changed the discipline by his erudite insistence that the *"faith" of Israel in YHWH* cannot and must not be separated from *the socioeconomic political realities* that the ancient community of Israel faced. Thus the covenantal vision of a neighborly economy, so clearly and frequently voiced in the Torah, is an advocacy for and an insistence upon both polity and practice that are pro-neighbor and anti-predation and accumulation.

It is my judgment that no leader of a Jewish or Christian community of faith can afford to disregard the gains accomplished by Gottwald in his interpretive work. Of course the Christian movement has been many centuries in becoming domesticated by the force of empire so that much of the church and its testimony are simply an echo and reiteration of dominant socioeconomic practice. As the church has readily settled for such domestication, it has lost much of its courage and its nerve, and its capacity to speak directly about the God who funds and inhabits the biblical and church traditions. The outcome is a church that is systemically anemic in its claim. As a result, the church has become a major champion and practitioner of "charity" that is content to remain safely inside the assumptions of confiscatory economics. Such an anemic practice provides neither energy nor courage for engagement in a neighborly economy that (a) requires *a radical sustained critique of our systemic economic arrangements* and (b) that *requires emancipated imagination about an alternative practice.* It is not necessary, in my judgment, that church leaders should be able to articulate the specificities of current economic reality and alternative prospects. It is enough if the church can fund and evoke imagination that gives a place to stand outside the current dominant system. That in turn requires, simply, that we learn to read the Bible differently, which is exactly what Gottwald sought to teach us. "Differently" is to see the linkage between *the character and resolve of God* and the *mandate of "sociopolitical equality"* as a function of Yahwism that is on offer everywhere in Scripture. Once one inhales the main gains of Gottwald's scholarship, one begins to see everywhere in Scripture a critique of dominant systems and the imaginings of a different "more excellent way."

No one doubts that Gottwald was a significant scholar. What is not to be missed amid his great learning, however, is that his tenacious life-long work is permeated with great moral passion. It is the passion he extended to the protesting students in Berkeley, but also to many other situations of injustice. He was a formidable voice in advocacy for feminism, and for native rights in the United States. This combination of erudition and social passion marks him as a presence among us of singular importance.

My purpose in writing this is to encourage pastors and church leaders who have lingered too long in old-fashioned historical criticism that they may have learned in seminary to do the work of study in the new directions of reading Scripture with reference to economic matters. On the one hand, such work belongs properly to the faithful church. That the gospel pertains to economic matters is evident in many Torah provisions to which the prophets often made appeal. And clearly Jesus was eventually executed by the state because he voiced a dangerous critique of and alternative to the dominant system of his day. Thus the recovery of faithful interpretation of the Bible is urgent among us.

On the other hand, as our society grows more frightened and more repressive, there is almost no room in our society for the voicing of restorative justice, the kind initiated by the Lord of the Exodus. The church, in its faithful reading and faithful preaching, is one such urgent venue for truth-telling that is now so needed among us. That truth-telling concerns the *exposé of our predatory economic system* that produces and sustains poverty via cheap labor; it also concerns *the articulation of an alternative* of "the way, the truth, and the life" that will yield neighborly abundance. As long as the church (and its pastors) is in unthinking collusion with dominant economic assumptions, this hard and transformative truth is not likely to be spoken aloud.

And how are they to believe in one of whom they have
never heard? And how are they to hear without someone to

proclaim him? And how are they to proclaim him unless they are sent? As it is written, "How beautiful are the feet of those who bring good news!" (Romans 10:14–15)

Gottwald understood that this is a time for "beautiful feet." His breathtaking book and his long refinement of it attest to a life that continues to matter to the rest of us—a good and faithful servant of the revolution and the God of the revolution!

28

ODE TO SAMMY

SAMMY, OUR CAT, came to us by way of rescue. He was a handsome, silky, loud-purring tabby. He was gregarious and mostly stayed in rooms where we were. At night he liked close bodily contact, while he purred into deep peaceable sleep. He died much too soon, and we are left with treasured memories and lingering sadness. I mention Sammy by way of introducing two pieces I have read lately concerning cats.

Quite by happenstance I have lately read *How to Live: A Life of Montaigne in One Question and Twenty Attempts at an Answer* by Sarah Bakewell (2010). The book is an introduction to and reflection upon the writing of the famous French essayist of the sixteenth century, Michael de Montaigne. Bakewell takes up Montaigne's essays concerning twenty answers she proposes to his governing question, "How to Live?" His essays are disciplined reflections and meditations on the specific quotidian reality of life all around him. He eschews speculative or abstract questions, including theological speculation.

Among his many whimsical investigations he considered the life of a cat (and a puppy!) in detail. He considered how the world looked to his cat and what his cat saw when it looked at him. He became aware that he and the cat had so much in common as each looked on the other and on the world. He also considered that he and the cat were very different because one can never know what another sees or notices. Thus he took his cat to be a partner in the act of specific observation of the world from a very specific perspective. Bakewell summarizes:

> *When you look at a puppy held over a bucket of water, or even at a cat in the mood for play, you are looking at a*

creature who looks back at you. No abstract principles are
involved; there are only two individuals, face to face, hoping
for the best from one another. (327)

Montaigne sees how much the two of them share and have in common.
The stark difference between them that he also notices is not only of
difference of species and genre. The difference is that each individual
sees and notices differently.

They looked at each other, and just for a moment, he leaped
across the gap in order to see himself through her eyes. Out of
that moment—and countless others like it—came his whole
philosophy. (328)

This is indeed the specificity of creation and of creatureliness taken with
utmost seriousness, refusing to be drawn away from its demanding
immediacy. Montaigne found the specificity of life embodied in his cat
to be overwhelming in its wonder, its otherness, and its commonality.
He wanted nothing more revelatory than that which was concretely in
front of him. In it he found answers to the question, "How to Live?"
The answer: "Life should be an aim unto itself, a purpose unto itself."

It is worth noting that Montaigne (1533–92) did his work in the
generation just preceding the birth of René Descartes (1596–1650).
Even though Descartes arrives just as Montaigne leaves the world, the
two of them are huge worlds apart. As it happened, dominant thought
and reasoning in the West has chosen to follow Descartes in his pursuit
of certainty through abstraction. He certainly would have had no
interest in the presence or perspective of a particular cat, not even
one belonging to Montaigne! That pursuit of certainty via abstraction
has resulted in what we call the modern world. It is mind-boggling
(and perhaps a yearning) to consider what might have eventuated if
the thought and reasoning of the West had chosen instead to pursue
Montaigne's practice of the specific and the quotidian. That, however,

never happened; for that reason we now are in a world propelled by ever new technologies of anxiety, fear, violence, and, consequently, greed.

When I read these words concerning Montaigne and his cat, I recalled that Martin Buber (in *I and Thou*) had in 1937 written of his cat in a not dissimilar fashion. (It is not clear whether Buber knew of Montaigne's essay, but it seems likely he might have.) Quite abruptly Buber introduces the thought:

> *An animal's eyes have the power to speak a great language. . . .*
> *The eyes express the mystery in its natural prison, the anxiety*
> *of becoming.* (96)

But then he becomes more specific:

> *Sometimes I look into a cat's eyes. The domesticated animal*
> *has not as it were received from us (as we sometimes imagine)*
> *the gift of the truly "speaking" glance, but only . . . to turn its*
> *glance to us prodigious beings. But with this capacity there*
> *enters the glance, in its dawning and continuing in its rising,*
> *a quality of amazement and of inquiry that is wholly lacking*
> *in the original glance with all its anxiety.* (97)

Now the cat has moved, in Buber's calculation, beyond "the anxiety of becoming" to be fully present in a glance:

> *The beginning of this cat's glance, lighting up under the touch*
> *of my glance, indisputably questioned me: "Is it possible that*
> *you think of me? Do you really not just want me to have fun?*
> *Do I concern you? Do I exist in your sight? Do I really exist?*
> *What is it that comes from you? What is it that surrounds*
> *me? What is it that comes to me? What is it?"* (97)

Buber's verdict on this momentary encounter concerns the "Thou" of the cat:

> *The world of* It *surrounded the animal and myself, for the space*
> *of a glance the world of* Thou *had shone out from the depths,*
> *to be at once extinguished and put back into the world of* It.

Thus Buber brings to this brief encounter all of his mystical anticipation and his readiness for the prospect of a "thou."

It is clear that Montaigne and Buber bring very different perspectives and expectations to their cats. Montaigne is thoroughly *practical, secular, and this-worldly*, with no hint of the religious. Buber by contrast is wholly *religious and mystical.* And yet the commonality between them is that both find their interactions with their cats to be *illuminating and dialogical.* For both of them the cat is a real, bodily, significant *other* who summons and addresses the alert human partner.

Beyond noting the parallels and the differences between Montaigne and Buber, it is most important that they shared wonder. What these two reports yield on the one hand is a full engagement with another member of the animal world. In that process there is a ready affirmation of the *commonality* between human creatures and these other creatures. On the other hand, the two reports indicate the hidden reality of the other so that even in a dialogic transaction there remains an *obscurity that allows for wonder* and that features *respect for the other* who remains not decoded in its difference.

Because our reflection on these cat encounters culminates in wonder, I may suggest one other aspect of this dialogic reality, namely, the ultimacy of glad, self-yielding praise. Of course "praise" is a symbolic act freighted with ultimacy that runs beyond Montaigne's strict this-world accent. But as Bakewell recounts (323–26), even Montaigne was subjected to religious rites at the end of his life. His engagement with these religious rites would have been devoid of every sectarian specificity, but perhaps he would not have denied the evocation of wonder, even for his this-worldly existence. That, I suggest, is sufficient grounds for judging that it is not inappropriate, at the end, to be left in "wonder, love, and praise."

On that basis I make reference to the avalanche of praise in Psalm 147 that mobilizes all of creation to refer beyond itself to the creator. That praise, until the final verse, is devoid of specificity; it settles for the sweep of wonder and awe as it summons all creatures to refer beyond themselves to the creator:

> *Praise the Lord from the earth,*
> *You sea monsters and all deeps,*
> *Fire and hail, snow and frost,*
> *stormy wind fulfilling his command!*
> *Mountains and all hills,*
> *fruit trees and all cedars!*
> *Wild animals and all cattle,*
> *creeping things and flying birds!* (vv. 7–10)

One can imagine all of these creatures (and others to be named later) joining in glad, grateful self-surrender to holiness beyond themselves. We might even add a few lines to the psalm:

> *Praise you domesticated pets,*
> *praise the creator, you cats along with dogs,*
> *praise you French secular cats,*
> *praise you Jewish mystical cats,*
> *praise you beautiful tabby cats from the Midwest.*
> *Let all cats declare their glad creatureliness in praise.*

And a final line:

> *Praise, you glad, furry, loud-purring well-beloved Sammy!*

God's first, best, most spoken language is Hebrew. That is why, when God looked upon the wonder of creation, God saw that it was *tov me'od* ("very good"). When God speaks cat-ese, I imagine that God may say of creation, "It is *purr-fect!*"

29

REFLECTIONS ON SOCIAL LOCATION

(In response to a query from my friend, Rabbi Nahum Ward-Lev)

IT IS NO great wonder that I have come down in the covenantal-Deuteronomic-prophetic trajectory of the Bible.

My dad, August, was a rural pastor who in the 1920s was educated at Eden Seminary in the social gospel. He was not outspoken about it, but that was no doubt his lens.

When I went to college, I majored under Th. W. Mueller, who was a one-man sociology department. He was a great advocate for social justice. I was in his class on "race" when the *Brown v. Topeka* decision was rendered. Austere as he was, he danced in class that day. (Richard Niebuhr, who long ago was president of the college, spoke at my commencement.)

When I went to Eden Seminary, my dad's school, most of my teachers were friends of the Niebuhrs. Richard long ago had been dean of the seminary. Reinhold was a long-time chair of the board of the seminary. Both retained a long-lasting relationship with the seminary. As a result, the Niebuhr brothers exercised a great influence on the seminary that was dubbed by some in our church as the "sociological" seminary. It was there that I was introduced to the Hebrew Bible and most especially to the prophets by my teachers, Allen Wehrli and Lionel Whiston Jr.

My graduate study at Union Seminary with James Muilenburg and Samuel Terrien urged me further into the prophets, most especially Muilenburg who in compelling ways performed Jeremiah. It was then that I got first access to Heschel on the prophets. He had once lectured at Eden Seminary, while I was a student there.

All of this was undergirded by my abiding indignation for the way in which my father was treated with economic parsimony by several of his congregations.

All of that, plus the fact that Deuteronomy contains the easiest Hebrew in the Bible!

30

REPRISE FOR SAMMY

SOME READERS MAY remember that I recently wrote about cats. My discussion included reference to our well-beloved tabby, Sammy, whom we have lost a while, Montaigne's secular cat, and Buber's Jewish cat. Of late I have read yet another compelling reference to cats.

I have been reading *The Uncontrollability of the World* (2020) by Hartmut Rosa, a German sociologist. Rosa takes as his thesis the proposition that a viable human world will be and must be ultimately uncontrollable in order that there can be free, honest, and authentic interaction. A capacity to reduce all of life to certitude would banish all mystery, all surprise, all openness, and all freedom. Rosa cites two cases of uncontrollability that make the point. First, the fall of snow is uncontrollable. We cannot initiate the fall of snow, nor can we stop it. It just happens, and we may be awed and surprised by it. Second, falling asleep is uncontrollable. We cannot will to fall asleep. Sleep comes upon us when it comes. Rosa, moreover, suggests that one's life depends upon "resonance" with another, and resonance depends upon the capacity of the other party to respond in freedom and agency. Complete control would inevitably reduce the other person to muteness, and there could be no genuine interaction at all.

And then, in the midst of his quite learned exposition, Rosa writes of his pet cat:

> *I experience her purring and trustfulness as events of genuine resonance precisely because she can also evade, because she sometimes* doesn't *purr, but scratches or even bites me—in short, precisely because I cannot completely control her. My*

> *argument is that, if I could make it snow at will, then I could*
> *never experience being called by the falling of snow. If my cat*
> *were a programmable robot that always purred and wanted*
> *to be cuddled, she would become nothing to me but a dead*
> *thing. (43–44)*

It is the agency of the other—falling snow, sleep, a cat—calling for me whereby I am impelled to response and engagement. It would be very different if the other were completely controlled.

> *It seems to me that there must be an aspect of* inherent
> uncontrollability *not only in our experiences or in our*
> *relationship to the world, but also* in things themselves, *if*
> *we are to be able to enter into a resonant relationship with*
> *them. (44)*

Once more he returns to his cat:

> *This is why, to come back to the example of the robotic cat,*
> *the uncontrollability inherent in any resonant relationship*
> *cannot be produced by a randomization program. If I were*
> *greeted in the evening not by my cat, but by a fluffy robot*
> *with big adorable eyes, a randomization program could well*
> *ensure that, on average, it would want to nuzzle and be*
> *petted by me nine times out of ten, while the other ten percent*
> *of the time it would hiss and run away from me. (46)*

Rosa sees that such a robot would allow for unpredictability, but

> *there would be no responsive relationship between the robot's*
> *behavior and my own. . . . I would know that it isn't trying*
> *to say anything to me, that it isn't even acknowledging me at*
> *all, that its behavior has nothing do with me. (46)*

In the end Rosa concludes that even the best-programmed robot could not enact the resonance that is essential for real, engaged interaction.

A society that lives in deep anxiety craves certitude. We seek to find such certitude by way of theological orthodoxy, or by scientific data, or by technological control, or by economic tyranny, or by a dozen alternative ideologies. Happily, none of these efforts can succeed because there is uncontrollability about our life. And this is because life at bottom is creatureliness sponsored by the creator God who wills a dialogical-covenantal relationship with God's own "other" who can never be reduced to an automaton. All of this full creatureliness is embodied in a cat—or in a snowflake, or even in the instance of sleeplessness. As Rosa judges,

> *We can only resonate with a counterpart that in a way*
> *"speaks with its own voice."* (47)

That "own voice" cannot be controlled. Our cats will not permit us to be ventriloquists who supply their speech, their purr, or their hiss. They will have their own say. And in having their own say, they are partners who purr and hiss themselves in our presence. We respond as we are able, as free in our response and our creatureliness as are they. Having *our say*, and resonating with the other who will have *a free say* is elemental to the will of the creator who calls us variously to our full creatureliness. And if, dear reader, this is not enough of cats for you, then check out the book by Rosa. It is a small volume, worth the effort. The book is a summons to engage knowingly the freedom that is constitutive of genuine creaturely existence.

31

UNDESERVING IN MICHIGAN

I REGULARLY READ the "Advice" column in our local paper, the *Record-Eagle*, written by Jeanne Philips. When I read it daily I sometimes sense an instance of *Schadenfreude* that someone has issues more complex than my own. More often I have a sense of incredulity; first, because of the complicated "pickles" in which people find themselves, or more often because very small "pickles" are escalated into big problems. Regularly, these several plaintiffs receive answers that are terse and to the point, most often good commonsense wisdom.

One such column caught my attention the other day because it came from Michigan, where I live. It was entitled "Non-Believer Credits Work, Not 'Blessings' for Success" (*Record-Eagle*, February 19, 2022). It was signed "Deserving in Michigan." The letter was from a woman with a "wonderful, well-paying job," sixteen years of happy marriage, a happy healthy daughter, and a stay-at-home husband/dad. The writer reports that she grew up in a "very religious family," but that she is "no longer religious" and does not attend church. She reports that she works "extremely long hours" and has "worked my butt off to get where we are."

The vexation about which "Deserving in Michigan" writes is her irritation that well-meaning people make "constant comments" that "you are so blessed to be where you are." She writes, "It feels wrong to equate my success to being blessed by God," when she has the strong sense that she herself, though thankful for the people who have helped her, is responsible for her wellbeing. She deserves her wellbeing and refuses the notion that her wellbeing is due to the blessing of God.

As we might expect, the answer to "Deserving in Michigan" from "Abby" (Jeanne Philips) is "Of course . . . you are deserving of your success." But do not engage in "braggadocio"; simply nod and let it go. That seems simple enough, just what I would have expected "Abby" to write. But even "Abby" agrees with "Deserving," that she is deserving, perhaps especially because she, like me, is from Michigan.

But of course "Deserving" poses a deep theological issue, one easily ignored by those of us who have "made it" in our competitive society. It would seem that "Deserving" is acutely unaware of or uninterested in those among us who are not so well off; perhaps she would judge that they are "undeserving," thus accepting the systemic injustice from which both she and I have benefited so much. Clearly any thoughtfulness would disclose to "Deserving" and the rest of us that the rewards of wellbeing do not come simply to the "deserving"; they come to the fortunate and the well-connected, especially to the fortunate and well-connected among us who are male, or white, or Western, or all the above. I have no wish to denigrate the letter writer; her letter is nonetheless an opportunity for us to reflect (1) on the way in which we are "deserving," (2) the way in which God's good gifts indiscriminately are given (Matthew 5:45), and (3) the way in which our sociopolitical system apportions those indiscriminately given gifts and so selects winners and losers. "Deserving" is unaware and uninterested in all of this. She speaks for a lot of us who have been narcoticized by the system not to notice how the system takes generous care of some of us and denies care to many of us. Her success, as for many of us, has numbed her to the social reality that lies behind her success. That social reality, moreover, remains willfully hidden until we make the effort to disclose it. With that social reality securely hidden from us, "Deserving" can readily imagine herself to be self-made.

Autonomy is a huge seduction for those of us who have prospered in an unjust system. Autonomy is the daring imagination that one's successful achievement makes one an independent self-starter who can enjoy self without a reference beyond the self. We can observe that seduction of autonomy is operative in many scriptural renderings.

Thus in the mock-song of Ezekiel, Pharaoh is charged with such illusionary autonomy:

> *My Nile is my own;*
> *I made it for myself.* (Ezekiel 29:3)

It is of course exactly the opposite. It is the Nile River that has made Pharaoh. It is the Nile that made possible the cultural sophistication and military prowess that permitted the dynastic line of pharaohs to be dominant figures for a long run of world history. Thus Pharaoh's words, put in his mouth by the prophet, constitute an act of self-delusion. In fact Pharaoh is quite penultimate, wholly dependent upon the "blessings" bestowed by the river. In his power and self-assurance Pharaoh was unable to acknowledge his penultimacy, and so he acts in hubris and imagines himself to be self-sufficient.

The same portrayal of self-delusion is evident in the familiar parable of Jesus (Luke 12:13–21). The farmer had land that "produced abundantly." He had no thought or care for either the land or the neighbor. He thought only of his own abundance. Indeed, there is no limit to how much abundance he is able to acquire and willing to store for himself. This great abundance, in his utter isolation, leads him to reflect on his future. He must ask himself what to do with his great accumulation:

> *What shall I do, for I have no place to store my crops?*

Then he decided:

> *I will do this: I will pull down my barns and build larger ones,*
> *and there I will store all my grain and my goods.* (v. 18)

Having done all of that to secure himself, he is wont to celebrate in self-congratulations:

> *Soul, you have ample goods laid up for many years:*
> *relax, eat, drink, and be merry.* (v. 19)

This portrayal of the man is a perfect model for a system of economic greed that sanctions accumulation without limit or restraint and without regard for anyone else. That by itself would be a sufficient delivery by the parable.

As we know, the parable does not end there. Instead the narrative introduces into the man's solitary world a new voice and a new agent, "But God said" (v. 20). This inexplicable, unexpected voice in the night promptly reduces the farmer to penultimacy. It places a decisive negative on his self-confidence, his hubris, and his sense that he "deserves" his abundance. No serious farmer would imagine that she is autonomous. Every serious farmer knows she is a creature of the land, and the land determines one's lot. It is only industrial agriculture, in the wake of Enlightenment autonomy, that could imagine limitless abundance kept for one's self as a viable way in the world. In the world of real agriculture, as in the rest of the real world, the true calculus is not one of "deserving," but one of gifts given to the just and the unjust.

In a world where the ideology of Pharaoh, the mentality of the parabolic farmer, and the self-understanding of "Deserving" in Michigan prevail, it is the work of the church to foster an alternative perspective that affirms that life is grounded in gifts generously given, and not in merit. In Lutheran dialect, this is simply the issue of "law and grace," but that simple either/or needs to be lined out in fresh ways in a culture that abounds in self-celebration and in endless promotion of self-esteeming individualism. The proper response to "Deserving" in her self-sufficiency and self-congratulations is the affirmation and offer of gifts graciously given that may evoke gratitude.

It is the work of the church to foster a practice and policy of thanks that bespeaks an honest penultimacy before the inscrutable ultimacy of the Holy God. Scripture everywhere gives voice to this truth for our lives. Below are some texts that have occurred to me.

In I Chronicles, David leads his people in gathering the offering of materials for the temple Solomon will build. Of this abundance he prays in thanksgiving:

*Riches and honor come from you, and you rule over all. In
your hand are power and might; and it is in your hand to
make great and to give strength to all. And now, our God, we
give thanks to you, and praise your glorious name. But who
am I, and what is my people, that we should be able to make
this freewill offering? For all things come from you, and of
your own have we given you.* (vv. 12–15)

David voices thanks. He articulates gratitude for himself and for his
people. He acknowledges that all his offerings are not other than a
return to God of God's own gifts. It is from this verse that we get the
familiar formulation for church offerings:

*We give thee but thine own, Whate'er the gift may be,
For all that we have is thine alone, A trust, O Lord, from thee.*

In I Corinthians 4:6 Paul writes pastoral advice to the church so that,

*. . . none of you will be puffed up in favor of one against
another.* (v. 6)

And then he poses a triad of searing questions to the church:

*For who sees anything different in you?
What do you have that you did not receive?
And if you received it, why do you boast as if it were not a gift?*
(v. 7)

The answer to the first question is that we can see nothing distinctive in the life or conduct of any of the members. The answer to the
second question is, "Nothing." They have nothing that has not been
given to them as a gift from God. The answer to the third question is,
"We boast because we have not accepted that what we have is a gift;

we have mistakenly come to regard what we have as an achievement, an accomplishment, or a possession of our own." These feeble answers permit us to draw only one conclusion: it is all gift! And because it is all gift, the only appropriate response is one of thanks that initiates a life of gratitude.

Psalm 116 provides a liturgical guide for thanks. On the one hand, thanks is a *verbal utterance* expressed, for example, in verses 8 and 16:

> *For you have delivered my soul from death,*
> *my eyes from tears,*
> *my feet from stumbling . . .*
> *O Lord, I am your servant;*
> *I am your servant, the child of your servant girl.*
> *You have loosed my bonds.*

Thanks is the actual utterance of the gifts, naming with specificity that for which we are grateful. The naming is a recognition that we are on the receiving end of that which we could not generate for ourselves. But second, thanks is an act of *glad yielding of something of value,* of giving from one's substance, an offering:

> *I will lift up the cup of salvation*
> *and call on the name of the Lord,*
> *I will pay my vows to the Lord in the presence of all his people. . . .*
> *I will offer to you a thanksgiving sacrifice*
> *and call on the name of the Lord.*
> *I will pay my vows to the Lord*
> *in the presence of all his people.* (vv. 13–14, 17–18)

The offering is an act of glad yielding of something of value in the awareness that it is not a gain to be counted, but a gift that mandates response.

It is the work of the church to nurture and evoke such *practices of thanks* that may issue in *lives of gratitude.* In a life of gratitude, the measure of "deserving" or "undeserving" simply becomes irrelevant. The center of our lives is reconfigured around generosity that need never be coerced, but is always glad and beyond limit or calculation. The competitive mindset of our economic system (that trickles into every facet of our lives) reduces everything to a *quid pro quo* measure. Gratitude, however, contradicts that logic. It affirms in active ways that the circulation of gifts, the sharing of goods, and the practice of generosity are never and can never be measured by a *quid pro quo* calculus. In the end, thanks is not just an attitude or a liturgical gesture. It is a way of being in the world, an active appreciative recognition that the gifts belong to all the neighbors, and that the presumably "deserving" are, willy-nilly, in full solidarity with the apparently "undeserving." It is no doubt the case that a life grounded in thanks will yield different neighbor practices and in different policies that upbuild the neighborhood.

For all our imagined autonomy, it is unsustainable. We finally must rely on generous gift-givers who, knowingly or not, reiterate the ultimate gift given—God's own life given for the sake of the world. And thus we may gladly say of ourselves, "We are blessed." We are blessed beyond measure by the self-giving of God. None of our illusions about being self-made or self-sufficient are finally persuasive. It is not that we "deserve." It is that we are on the receiving end of a richness of blessing, mediated through thanks-filled lives, ultimately from the God of all gifts. So we act out blessings, share them, and thereby refuse the self-regard of Pharaoh and the illusion of the rich, beguiled farmer of the parable. We know better than that, so we may live better than that!

CONCLUSION

THE TASK OF theological interpretation is demanding and urgent in our society. We do such work amid the fierce insistence of ideologies of nationalism and racism on the one hand, and at the edge of vacuous technological reductionism on the other. In such a contest it is no small matter to insist, according to the confession of the church, that our lives and the life of all creation stand before the Holy One who is our creator and redeemer. These ideologies and this reductionism seek, as best they can, to bracket out any thought of the Holy One who matters in any decisive way to the life of the world.

Our interpretive task is to insist otherwise. Indeed, I have characterized "prophetic imagination" as the act of imagining the God of the Gospel as a real character and a lively agent in the midst of God's own creation. Such a claim is an affront to our modern/postmodern rationality. It is, moreover, a scandal to a church that specializes in more-or-less sentimental "pastoral care." But we face the reality of all of these efforts in ideology, reductionism, or sentimentality, each of which leaves us on our own and at risk as the *ultimate* in the world. For better or worse, the claim of the Anthropocene is that human persons are now the measure of reality. Thus we are left without resources beyond ourselves and without restraints beyond our own resolve.

We insist otherwise! We insist, in our interpretive work, that the human enterprise is *penultimate*; it derives from and is answerable to an agency that is well beyond us or our control. We can notice the awkward embarrassment of the church in making such a claim when we pay attention to the prayers of the church that mostly lack the energy of conviction, or when the hymns of the church are mostly marked by horizontal romanticism. So to make a big statement of "otherwise," I appeal to the old hymn of Isaac Watts, now lost to us through disuse. I cite it as a contrast to most of our very circumspect contemporary prayers and hymns:

> *Before Jehovah's awful throne,*
> *Ye nations bow with sacred joy;*
> *Know that the Lord is God alone,*
> *He can create and he destroy,*
> *He can create, and He destroy.*
>
> *His sov'reign pow'r, without our aid,*
> *Made us of clay, and formed us men;*
> *And when, like wand'ring sheep we strayed,*
> *He brought us to His fold again,*
> *He brought us to His fold again.*
>
> *We are His people, we His care,*
> *Our souls, and all our mortal frame;*
> *What lasting honors shall we bring,*
> *Almighty Maker, to Thy name,*
> *Almighty Maker, to Thy name?*
>
> *We'll crowd Thy gates with thankful songs,*
> *High as the heavens our voices raise;*
> *And earth, with her ten thousand tongues,*
> *Shall fill Thy courts with sounding praise,*
> *Shall fill Thy courts with sounding praise.*
>
> *Wide as the world is Thy command,*
> *Vast as eternity Thy love;*
> *Firm as a rock Thy truth must stand,*
> *When rolling years shall cease to move,*
> *When rolling years shall cease to move.*
>
> (*The Evangelical Hymnal* [1922], 64)

(I had to go back to a much earlier hymnal in my tradition to find this hymn, as it is absent in more recent hymnals.) There are many reasons why we don't sing this hymn. The issue of objectionable patriarchal language is evident. The initial use the term "awful" seems to speak of divine violence. All of that is to be promptly acknowledged. But apart from such objections, I suspect the deeper reason we have neglected this hymn is its singular insistence that this Holy God can act in trans-formative ways, in judgment and in restoration. The hymn does not end in fear or anxiety. It ends rather in confidence in God's love that is as "vast" as eternity. The hymn permits the church to voice its trust in the lively, attentive rule of God in the life of the world.

It is in such a world of the Holy One—an awkward embar-rassment to us—that we do our interpretive work that insists upon our own penultimacy before the agency of God, an agency that has to do with real life in the real world. We may be dazzled that we are able to do this good work at all, feeble and frail as we all are. It is mind-boggling to me to think that everywhere across the landscape of our society, the church (with its allies in the synagogue) continues the work of interpretation, thus refusing virulent ideologies, technological reductionism of the mystery of our life, and easy sentimentalisms. It is good work; it is, moreover, urgent work for the sake of our common humanness and our common creatureliness with all of God's other well-beloved creatures. I am glad to pass along these thoughts of mine in the hope that they may be a source of encouragement for the host of those who continue the good work.